Courage To Conquer

Passing the Sword to the Last Generation

Courage To Conquer
Passing the Sword to the Last Generation
by
Lester Sumrall

Harrison House
Tulsa, Oklahoma

Courage To Conquer —
Passing the Sword to the Last Generation
ISBN 0-89274-867-2
Copyright © 1992 by Lester Sumrall
Evangelistic Association
P. O. Box 12
South Bend, IN 46624

Published by Harrison House, Inc.
P. O. Box 35035
Tulsa, OK 74153

I dedicate this book to the end-time leaders who face the greatest challenges and the greatest opportunities in the history of the world.

> And it shall come to pass in the last days, saith God, I will pour out of my Spirit upon all flesh: and your sons and your daughters shall prophesy, and your young men shall see visions, and your old men shall dream dreams.
>
> Acts 2:17

Contents

A Special Word From the Author

Are you a pastor? An evangelist? How about a missionary? An assistant pastor? An associate pastor? A lay person? The Lord has a call for you. It is found in John 15:16: **Ye have not chosen me, but I have chosen you....** Those are very strong words.

You have been called.

The Bible says that God has set in the Church apostles and prophets, pastors, teachers and evangelists. God set these special people in the Church. But every born-again child of God has a commission to take the Gospel to every human being.

When I visit some missionaries, I just shake my head in sadness. They have gone off to the mission field without a clear leading from God that this is where they are to go. They intend to do well, to show their love for God, but they don't wait for Him to tell them where they are to go. They just go.

The Bible says that God does the choosing. He sees potential when no one else does — more than our friends and family. He sees the end from the beginning. He does the choosing. Countries today send out ambassadors to other nations. Ambassadors do not apply for the job. They are chosen by the government to represent their country. You and I are chosen in the same way — by God.

Jesus Christ, the Head of the Church, said, "I want you to represent Me on the earth." Think of how precious and awesome that is — that God, Who created all things including man, would choose you to represent Him on earth. He sees something in *you*. That's what this book is about.

Some time ago, I spoke to the Livets Ord School for Pastors in Uppsala, Sweden, and presented much of what I have to say in this book. Indeed, that vital message is scattered throughout these pages. If you were in attendance, you will recognize that it is virtually the outline of this book and that its clear message is recounted in several key chapters.

For example, the story of my very disillusioning teenage ordination into the ministry — and the lessons I learned from it — is told in detail in Chapter 12. We look at how some great leaders and generals bade farewell to their troops when we get to Chapter 24. Then, an important lesson that the Lord showed me about the difference between the North Star and shooting stars is recounted in Chapter 25.

But the important verse for you to consider right now is John 15:16. Translated loosely from the original Greek, it proclaims, ''It was not you who picked Me out, but I Who chose you and appointed you.'' The *King James Version* says: **Ye have not chosen me, but I have chosen you, and ordained you....** What does that mean?

Read on, my friend!

Foreword

Beyond the pleasure and privilege of writing this foreword are the blessings and benefits of knowing Lester Sumrall, a many-talented man.

Lester Sumrall has earned the right to counsel young candidates for the ministry. I would not know any phase of the ministry in which he is not experienced. Like Luke's comment about the Master, this book relates to . . . **all that Jesus began both to do and teach** (Acts 1:1).

Today, the need is for "combat men." Too many assigned have never built a church, cast out a devil or raised a budget. Mark trained under Barnabas. Timothy trained under Paul. Lester Sumrall approaches the podium with a half-century of experience gained in school rooms around the world.

Like me, he is a Gospel preacher. It is the Gospel that is unexcelled by any message on the planet. It, in an alchemy of its own, transforms mankind. Secular knowledge is inadequate. At best, it can only be auxiliary. Lester Sumrall finds a new emphasis for this truth.

The author has never let himself become dated. He moves with the times in application and available instruments. He knows how to use electronics effectively. The fire and passion for preaching both still burn within him and are evident in the pulpit and on camera.

There is a well of sympathy in Lester Sumrall. He wants young preachers to succeed. He spends time with them. His own, considerable beginning days are always before him. He will not forget you. He is a friend. I wish him well in this volume. If together and with the prayers of many we are able to usher in a new hour of effective evangelism, this will crown our lives and ministries.

You will discover early, as you absorb this new text, that Lester Sumrall believes that enduement, unction and illumination cannot be taught. These, which make preaching effective, are issues provided by the Holy Spirit. Above all, Lester Sumrall seeks at all times this anointing. I wish him a multiplication of his own ministry through those he will train.

Dr. C. M. Ward

Preface

I am a young man who was much younger (and greener) when I came under the ministry of Dr. Lester Sumrall. Over the years of our friendship, I have had many occasions to identify with the young man we read of in the sixth chapter of 2 Kings. In this scripture, a young minister lost an ax head while cutting down a tree, and he relied on the man of God to retrieve the ax head.

Dr. Sumrall has been the retriever of lost ax heads for many years, and more than once he has restored the sharp edge of my ministry. To the rest of the world, my bravely pounding the tree with a headless ax handle may have sounded genuine, but it never fooled Dr. Sumrall. He always seemed to know when the bite was missing from my bark, and he always seemed to know just what to say or do to restore the edge to my ministry. It is my hope and prayer that this book will restore your sharpness, also.

The first time I had the privilege of being under Dr. Sumrall's ministry, I felt a sense of destiny. I knew in my spirit that my future ministry would be greatly influenced by him. From that day, I had a strong desire to meet Dr. Sumrall. On occasion, I would be standing no more than a few feet from him, but I did not presume to introduce myself. King David said that of all the sins of his life (including adultery and murder), his greatest sin was the sin of presumption.

It is my strong conviction that a man's gift will make room for him. I purposed that if, as I believed, God had tied my destiny to Dr. Sumrall, then God would bring us together. No matter how much I wanted to speak first, I held my peace. In due season, Dr. Sumrall initiated the contact between us. From the beginning, our relationship has been that of a spiritual father to a spiritual son. When God does something, it is always on time, in good taste and according to His plan.

A true friend is not just someone who congratulates us when we are right, but who also corrects us when we are wrong or in danger of going wrong. One of the most important times I have ever spent with Dr. Sumrall was a time of correction and stern instruction.

One day Dr. Sumrall told me to sit down opposite him. He then pulled his chair to the point that our knees were touching. He next shared something that he perceived in the spirit about my life and ministry. Some things I will not share here, but one thing he dealt with me about was ministry and materialism. He looked into my face and said, "Before you leave this room, decide whether you want to be rich or have God's best."

This is not intended to be a criterion for anyone else's ministry. It was God speaking to me. I have been blessed more than anyone I know. My needs have always been met with abundance, but wealth has never been my goal from that day to this. Dr. Sumrall has affected my life in so many ways that it is difficult to isolate which ones were the most important. My wife and I were privileged to have Dr. Sumrall lead us in our wedding vows. The anointing and leading of the Spirit in that wedding ceremony have blessed thousands who have viewed the wedding on video tape. With Dr. Sumrall, a wedding is much more than a collection of dusty vows out of some book. Our wedding ceremony was as alive and vital as Dr. Sumrall himself.

I will never forget his teaching that a truly godly marriage is one that takes place on three levels: spirit, soul and body. He taught us that most marriages are merely a physical attraction. Many are a union of just body and mind; others are a union of mind, will and emotions (the three areas of the soul) and the body. Of these three types of unions, 50 percent will end in divorce. Very few marriages are three dimensional — with spirit, soul and body — but these are the marriages that stand the test of time.

At one point in the reciting of the vows, Joni was required to say, "as God gives me grace," and Dr. Sumrall said, "It's going to take God." That statement has been the strength of our marriage. We realize that our strength comes from God.

During the first year of our marriage, the pressures on my wife and me were tremendous. We traveled over a hundred nights, including several trips abroad. We were also constructing a 5,200-seat sanctuary during this same time. A month after our wedding, my wife and I went with Dr. Sumrall to Sweden. During this trip, my wife became very ill and was stressed to the breaking point.

During one of the evening services, Dr. Sumrall stopped in the middle of his sermon and said to my wife, "Joni, stand up." He proceeded to speak by the Spirit: "I have called you to do this, and don't ever be discouraged and say again, 'This is not for me.'" That prophecy has seen my wife through many a day filled with the pressure of ministering with me. Since my wife and I are one flesh, that strength imparted to her means more to me than words can state.

I said earlier that God orchestrated the union of my ministry to Dr. Sumrall. I will never forget the day that I was driving to Lane Aviation in Columbus, Ohio, to pick up Dr. Sumrall. I had seen such power and gifts operating through his ministry that I fully believed he could look inside me and see anything in my heart and life. His gaze was so piercing, and he seemed to see everything that was happening in the spirit realm.

As I drove to pick him up, I feverishly prayed, "God, if there is anything wrong in my heart, please reveal it to me first, and I will deal with it right now." As much as Dr. Sumrall has meant to the development of my ministry, I know he will mean even more to me in the future, as I receive fresh instruction from his life and words, and as I fondly remember such times that are past.

Rod Parsley, Senior Pastor
World Harvest Church
Columbus, Ohio

Introduction:
Take This Self-Test

Are you fighting God's call? Try this little test:

____ Do you often repeat to yourself the excuse that you are a "good person" or even a good preacher and that someone else will have to deal with all the problems that you see in the world?

____ Do visiting worship leaders irritate you when they challenge you to wake up, jump out of your pew and begin praising the Lord? Do you wish they would calm down — or that you could go home?

____ Are you disgusted with yourself for listening to scandalous whispers about preachers, maybe fellow ministers, especially those who in the past fervently challenged you to do more for Jesus Christ?

____ Are you unsettled by memories of little old ladies who proclaimed a personal word from the Lord for you, particularly that God has chosen for you a miraculous life of evangelism and teaching?

____ In the secret solitude of your deepest fears, do you wonder what would happen if you really began listening to the loving, guiding voice of the Holy Spirit?

____ Are you hurting inside, tired of trying to do anything but obey the Lord's quiet, urgent demands on your life?

____ Are you miserable as you follow your own ambitions? As you do so, are your big dreams souring? Have they turned out to be empty promises, luring you into unfulfillment and frustration?

17

_____ Are you tired of playing it safe? Would you like to have the backbone to follow your strong, but suppressed, convictions? Are you ready to step out in faith and trust God to help you fulfill your vision?

If you answered even one of those questions yes, praise God, my friend. Maybe you can avoid the shock therapy that God had to use on a preacher named Jonah. If you remember, he attempted to ignore his call. However, he ended up preaching anyway while smelling like something that must have attracted a lot of cats.

Are you running from God's plan for you?

Well, I ran, too.

Part I
Are You Running
From Your Calling?

1
God Wants You

I have an urgent message for you. It may change your life. So, these humorous and dramatic — but true — stories that I am going to tell you may be dangerous.

How?

They are intended to threaten your easy lifestyle. This message may even wreck your view of Christianity. Maybe you should put this book down right now — before any damage incurs!

God wants you.

He wants me to help you shake off your safe Christian lifestyle and your Sunday morning business-as-usual attitude. He wants you to begin irritating — yes, irritating — a modern Church that doesn't want to think about Jesus Christ or the extreme penalty of sin.

Through God's grace over the years, I have acquired many titles. I have been called doctor, college president, author, magazine editor, pastor and broadcasting network president. But above everything else, I am a preacher — a traveling revivalist. And in my travels, I want you to know that the Church I see today is a weak and flabby imitation of the New Testament Church. Powerless Christianity doesn't threaten Satan.

Jesus wants me to proclaim that God wants you. We live in times where that message is like food to the starving. Our world longs for a ray of hope. And here it is: *God wants you.*

We live in an era unlike any other in the history of mankind. There is such opportunity for spreading the life-changing Gospel of Jesus Christ! So many doors have been thrown open worldwide! In America, the message is just as needed. Our lives must be a witness that Jesus Christ indeed makes a positive difference.

As the late David du Plessis once said, *God has no grandchildren.* That means that I cannot get into heaven just because my mother was a great and faithful prayer warrior. It means that you cannot expect to be saved just because your father is a good Christian man.

You Must Be a Child of God

The relationship must be between you and the Almighty Creator of the Universe! You need to see Him answering your prayers. You need to experience His mighty peace. You need to hear His gentle voice telling you what to do with your life. You need to know Him, to seek Him, to depend on Him, to be afraid to turn away from Him. You need to know that He is your only Source.

He wants you.

When you seek out the personal, peaceful, powerful presence of the mighty Maker of All Things, you will never want to leave. He is truth. He loves you. God is alive, and He loves you more than you can imagine.

Don't expect Him to take orders from you. You and He will never be equals. He enjoys your worship and expects your obedience. He will tell you no when you ask Him for things that He does not deem appropriate. He's in charge. He likes you. Yes, He loves you — but He also *likes* you. There is a difference, you know. He approves of you. After all, He made you. And He has great plans and hopes for you. He has a call for you, a purpose. It is different with each of us.

Have You Decided To Be a Preacher?

Maybe you haven't obeyed your call yet — but you are feeling a strong, gnawing urging on your life. Hallelujah! I happen to believe that every Christian should be a minister. The Bible says that we are all members of a royal priesthood. (1 Pet. 2:9.) We all have a call on our lives. Given the pagan condition of our country and the world, it's going to take all of us.

Serving Jesus is exciting. If you have not yet experienced it, one of the most incredible fulfillments in life is when you lead somebody to Jesus Christ. You can't do it out of guilt. You can't effectively lead anybody to Christ just because it's your duty. You have to want that individual to be spared from hell. You have to want him to have happiness here on earth. You can't change lives just because some book says you ought to do it, either. No, God wants you.

He Wants Your Willingness

God wants you to *want* to serve Him. He has a plan for you — and it's not for you to sit around, content that you are the son or daughter of somebody who was a good Christian or that you are a successful pastor with a very content flock, a balanced budget and a master's degree hanging on your wall. No, God has more for you. He has a mighty purpose for you. He wants you to get out there and *change lives*, to make your world a better place. He wants to commune with you, too, to hear your praise and worship. He has built within you a yearning for Him.

Today America is hurting. All around you is opportunity to help those who have deep spiritual and physical needs. This gnawing personal darkness is not just an American phenomenon. I see it when I go to England — that historically mighty power for world evangelism. I see it in virtually godless Switzerland and Sweden and the

Netherlands, and certainly in Germany and France and even Italy — where dynamic Christian missionary efforts are underway as I write this.

Maybe That's Your Call — Missions

Why should we send missionaries to Italy? To Switzerland? To Holland?

To claim back these mighty birthplaces of our heritage.

With the insecurities of national economies all over the globe, people are searching for answers. They are hungering and thirsting after truth. They want a lifestyle that works. They want answers. We know that only one Way works.

God wants you to help them find the One Who can protect them and provide for them when everyone else is starving in the wilderness. He wants you to tell them about the time He used ravens to bring food to Elijah in the middle of a terrible drought — and how the widow's oil jar never went empty because she trusted God. (1 Kings 17:9-16.) He wants you to live in complete dependence on Him. He wants *you.* He wants others to see what a difference He makes in your life.

2
I Want To Pass the Sword to You

When I was a little boy, I did not see anything special in preachers or Christians.

Since my mother thought evangelists were great, we always seemed to have some parson visiting in our home or eating dinner with us or staying all night with us. They always got the really good food and took over *my* bed — forcing me to sleep on a quilt on the floor. I did not appreciate it. I retaliated by stealing from their pockets while they slept. It was quite profitable even though often they had as little as three dollars to their name.

I'd tinker with their old rattletrap cars, too, so the junkpiles wouldn't run in the morning. Once I even shot out the lights of a revival tent while everybody slept. *It was a big mystery.* Even the sheriff was baffled. I was too young to be suspected.

I was not a Christian.

One day when I was still in grade school, I got so angry at a visiting parson with a particularly large family that I jumped his goody-two-shoes son. The pasty-faced kid was about my age — and I poured molasses into his hair. Then, as I held the squealing little preacher's boy down in the dirt, I dumped flour on his head and rubbed in the gooey mess. I cussed the kid but good, warning him, ''Now, you go tell your father to get out of here and leave us alone.''

But instead of leaving, the revivalist just called for special fasting and prayer. He challenged the entire church to pray for Lester. That really irked me. The whole revival meeting turned its attention to trying to get poor Mrs. Sumrall's delinquent son saved. Then my mother got up and told of her vision that I would be a great preacher. It was terrifying. I was quite content with being the Huckleberry Finn of my community — not some sissy. I liked to cuss, steal and skinny dip! I certainly didn't see myself as a preacher with an undertaker's suit, soft hands, a benign smile, and a group of old biddies gathered around me discussing the flower arrangement for the altar.

No, I was a *man*, not some pansy. I wasn't sure whether I wanted to go out West and be a gold-mining gunslinger — or head East and be a banker-oilman-tycoon. In any case, I intended to be rich. *Preachers were not.* They were dainty little fellows who owned nothing and couldn't succeed at anything else — that's what I believed.

Of course, that's a lie straight out of hell. Sure, I know a few preachers like that — sweet guys who don't have any particular ambition. They seem to like the idea of hiding in the safe, holy sanctuaries of churches — preaching pretty funerals and lovely weddings and weekly fifteen-minute sermonettes filled with pleasant inspiration.

Students with such misconceptions occasionally show up at Bible college, and I shake my head in wonder. I hope the school will build a fire under them. But I know I must train preachers with a blazing fire in their belly — hungry young zealots, impatient to claim the entire world for Jesus!

God wants *you!*

I pray for Christians who are interested in trying to understand this simple phrase: *God wants you.*

I have something else to share with you. I deeply desire to *''pass the sword''* to you. What does that mean? A hurting, empty world is out there, desperately needing Jesus Christ. Until I draw my last breath, I must do my very best to reach those who have not yet heard. One way my ministry can continue even after I am gone, though, is this: *I want to pass the sword to you.*

I am convinced that these next years will be some of the most crucial in the history of the Church. You will face challenges unheard of before. But with the challenges will come unlimited opportunities as the power and grace of God is poured out in unprecedented ways.

Some time ago, God spoke to me that I was to teach the spiritual leaders of the coming generation about:

* Humble living
* Spiritual instruction
* My own unusual experiences in His service
* Prayer

Why? So that the generation that follows me can benefit from some of my experience. So that you won't have to make all the mistakes I made. So you can avoid some pitfalls that I have fallen into.

While preaching in Brazil some time ago, I had been fasting for three weeks. Standing there I said, ''Lord, show me my end.''

He responded instantly, ''It is in Psalm 71:18.''

I opened my Bible to read the passage and laughed aloud. It said, **Now also when I am old and gray-headed. . . .**

I had to chuckle. But I quickly learned two things:

1. That I was to get old, whatever that is. By the time you read this, I will have passed my eightieth birthday, and perhaps then I will start feeling old. However, I doubt it; and

2. That I was to get gray headed. Well, the last time I looked in the mirror, it had already happened.

But that wasn't all the Lord wanted me to get from Psalm 71:18. What does the rest of the verse say? . . .**O God, forsake me not; until I have shewed thy strength unto this**

generation, and thy power to every one that is to come.
In the more modern *New King James Version*, it reads,
...Until I declare Your strength to this generation, Your
power to everyone who is to come.

God was saying to me, "I want to reveal My glory. Tell
young preachers how I can supply their needs, large or
small, and teach the people to praise Me for My greatness."
So that's it.

That's what I'm supposed to do.

It is wonderful to know the type of work you are to
do until the end of your life. I asked God regarding my end,
and He described it for me. So, I had better obey — and
thus, this book. I want to be able to declare like the Apostle
Paul, **I have fought a good fight, I have finished my course,
I have kept the faith** (2 Tim. 4:7). I'm to teach the young
ministers and church leadership that God's power is real,
that it can be attained and that they should teach His power.

So, what shall I leave with you? Well, when Jesus
readied to leave earth, He told His apostles in Mark 16:15:
...Go ye into all the world, and preach the gospel to every
creature. That goes for you, too. That command was meant
for *all* of us.

3

Jesus Wants To Be Your Lord

Once when traveling the countryside with His disciples, Jesus asked: "Who do people say the Son of Man is?"

You can read what happened in Matthew 16:13-20. The fishermen, former tax collectors and religious zealots who made up His disciples answered according to what they had been hearing other people say. None of them would stick his neck out! In the crowds, they had heard some people speculate that Jesus was John the Baptist. Others believed He was Elijah, Jeremiah or one of the other prophets returned from the dead. So, that's how the disciples answered.

But I want you to examine carefully Jesus' next question. Notice how disappointed He was with their answers. Why? Because His disciples only reported what others were saying. So, Jesus followed up with a simple question: "And you, who do you say that I am?"

Peter responded — declaring what today is called the "good confession" that Jesus is the Son of the living God. (v. 16.) Jesus' reaction was just as historic, proclaiming in verse 18-20 that Peter — *Petros* or "rock" — was the rock upon which He would build His Church! Peter's life was never again the same.

Today, many people offer opinions about Jesus — cerebral, intellectual, theological, theoretical, academic answers straight from books or a cassette tape.

But even non-Christians can do that!

29

Some who do not know Him proclaim with polite deference that they regard Him as a great teacher — or an important cultural figure in the evolution of Western civilization. Some nuts claim that He was an extraterrestrial — a UFO spaceman borne to earth aboard the chariots of the gods! You may laugh at that, but some Christian opinions about Jesus have even less basis in truth. He has become a plastic good-luck charm on the dashboard or a mystical baby with a halo to whom singing drummer boys cut best-selling record albums.

Perhaps to you He is a mystical figure from a Cecil B. DeMille movie, complete with misty silhouette, miraculous robe and a pained facial expression prompting angelic choirs to begin crescendoing classical music!

Such answers reveal our human shallowness, our immaturity and our pitiful superficiality. But here is something worse. To so many, Jesus is nothing more than a Son of God, Savior, Prince of Peace, King of Kings, Lord of Lords. He is just a cliche.

Nice words without any meaning.

To others, He is the great sugar daddy in the sky — the mighty gift-giver! Is He merely the Way, the Truth, the Light, to you? Is He a kind and giving Son of God Who offers salvation, but demands nothing from you in return?

I want you to understand, He has a very definite demand on you: *Jesus wants you.*

He Awaits Your Answer!

So, please, don't give me any more traditional platitudes! No more cliches. Intellectual citations and quoted seminary texts are merely what others think.

Today consider this personal, direct question from your Lord and Savior: *"You, who do you say that I am?"*

Who is He to you? Is He merely a tradition? A continuation of family culture? Is He your obedience to the great American way? You are not a Buddhist or a Satanist, so you must be a Christian? Is He merely a stranger on an ancient cross, killed 2,000 years ago for reasons that are an absolute puzzle to you? Don't be afraid to admit such doubts or hurts.

Just like the disciples that day, all believers must answer. Standing alone before Almighty God, we cannot evade. We must face the judgment of God.

Your answer is vital. Here is what God requires: *Jesus Christ must become the Lord of your life.*

4

What Does "Jesus Is Lord of Your Life" Mean?

Is the statement *"Jesus Christ must become the Lord of your life!"* just religious gobbledygook to you?

If you are already a preacher — you may be so jaded to religious cliches that you are finding it easy just to skim over such a phrase. So, what does it mean?

Is Jesus Lord of Your Life?

Are the words nonsensical? How *can* Jesus be the Lord of your life?

When Jesus truly becomes your Lord, you will change in subtle and radical ways. You will begin a relationship with the Creator, the One Who made everything, the King of the universe.

Here's the great part. This new relationship fulfills a great hunger God put within each of us. It pushes buttons deep within our inner being, giving us peace that passes understanding, joy unspeakable and the ability to love those who treat us terribly. It fulfills one of our reasons for existing.

God created us to be His friends and children — for us to benefit from His great companionship and to enjoy His generous blessings. The desire for Him to be our Lord is stitched into our fabric, engraved into our hearts and inscribed on our blueprints. It has been part of His plan since far before the foundation of the world.

In order to understand the real significance of the Lordship of Christ, it helps to understand the meaning of the word "lord" and the significance of its opposite — "servant."

In the original Greek, Matthew 18:23-35 tells of a lord who had a servant who owed him a lot of money. The story says that the boss forgave the servant's debt. However, he abruptly changed his mind when the servant was not similarly merciful with another servant who owed him a much smaller amount. Angrily, the lord ordered the servant to be sold as well as his wife and children and all that he had.

This kind of servant was the property of the lord. He and his wife and children were slaves! They were human beings who could be bought and sold. They were the property of another person, owned by him. They had lost all rights, privileges, possessions, liberty, self-will, self-determination and even personal identity.

Such slave families could be dissolved at the whim of the owner — children sold when they were marketable, husbands or wives put on the auction block to raise cash for the owner. They were considered inferior beings and were not paid wages, but were usually given clothes, room and board.

The slave had to serve his lord without any conditions. He could not quit or put any stipulations on his master.

Read Luke 17:7-10, 2 Corinthians 11:20, Galatians 4:22 and Philippians 1:1 to get another perspective on servanthood.

In contrast to the slave, a bond servant was free to quit but *chose* to stay and serve his master. He was paid wages but he was more than a mere hireling — working only for money. Such an individual was greatly devoted to the human lord. He had a free will, but would not take any action that would harm his boss. He so respected his lord that he submitted voluntarily to his directions. This sort of person is not pleased unless the boss is pleased. This is the classic company man, the committed employee whose identity has blended with that of the firm.

What Kind of Servant Are You?

God gives you a free will. You can leave His Lordship and return to a life of sin and independence if you choose. You may begin as a mere servant, but may find yourself voluntarily taking on the role of a slave. The Apostle Paul frequently called himself a slave of Jesus Christ — bought for a price.

As I count my many blessings, as I thank the Lord for saving me from myself and giving me wondrous new life, I find my heart bursting with a need to serve Him. Willingly, I became a slave, answering a deep, urgent call on my life to preach.

As you answer such a call, you may feel the need to place your life before your great and mighty Lord as an offering and sacrifice. Joyfully you will choose to become a slave, unprotesting, filled with peace and thanksgiving, serving the only Lord Who meets your needs, Who saved your soul, Who is preparing a mansion for you in eternity, and in Whose service you experience your only deep and lasting fulfillment.

The Lordship of Christ means that we stop living for ourselves — giving up our selfish, lonely, egotistical lives — entering a life of service to Him, a lifestyle of bond servanthood, dependent on His will always.

This was the call of Christ to His disciples: ...**"If anyone wishes to come after Me, let him deny himself, and take up his cross daily, and follow Me"** (Luke 9:23 NAS). That is the call to the Lordship of Christ. Saying "Jesus is Lord" means that He is your owner and that you are His humble, obedient slave.

Upon paying the price for us, Jesus became our owner to such a degree that "we are not our own." (1 Cor. 6:19-20.) When we give ourselves to Him, He gets all that we are — spirit, soul and body — and everything that we possess — material goods, talents, education, earthly position. He has all rights over us! Our thoughts must be laid down before Him. (2 Cor. 10:4-5.) We become mere administrators or "stewards" of our lives and possessions — caretakers of all that He puts in our hands, according to 1 Peter 4:10 — and have a responsibility to take good care of His possessions.

However, in Matthew 7:21, Jesus said: **"Not everyone who says to me, 'Lord, Lord,' will enter the kingdom of heaven, but only he who does the will of my Father who is in heaven"** (NIV).

Are you willing to do that?

To find out, take this little test.

5

Take this "Personal Relationship Test"

Today many preach a Gospel without commitment, a rose-colored Gospel in which God gives all without asking anything in exchange.

So, it is time to ask: *Do you have a personal rapport with Jesus?* If not, what should you do about it? A good place to start is with a confession of your mouth: *"Jesus is my Lord."*

Are you prepared to make this confession with all your heart? Is Jesus your Lord and Savior? *Then speak it aloud! Right now! Declare it! "Jesus is Lord!"*

But surrendering your life to Jesus and accepting Him as your Lord is only part of what you must do as a Christian to live under this Lordship. The Lordship of Christ must be lived each day, each hour, each minute of your life. It is as important as breathing.

Many believers find it difficult to live under the Lordship of Christ. Many are victims of frustration and discouragement. Often this is caused by a false understanding of the way in which the Lord rules in the life of the believer. It is necessary, then, that we understand that in order for the Lordship of Christ to become real, we must voluntarily and consciously surrender to His ownership.

This means more than good intentions. We've got to take specific actions. We must separate ourselves from the world, from its scheme of thinking and from the values that govern it.

In Romans 12:1,2 we are told that:

* We are to present our bodies as a living sacrifice, holy, acceptable to God. This must be done rationally, with thought, with meditation, based on a conscious decision.

* We are to cease thinking with the mindset of the world. That is, we are not to conform ourselves to the world. On the contrary, we are to renew our minds according to the will of God. We must trust and obey Him even when our natural senses tell us to do otherwise.

If we are to experience the Lordship of Christ, daily we must evaluate our lives according to the Word of God, in an attitude of prayer. We must ask if we are being subject to the Lord. Our doing this gives God the liberty of speaking to us, allowing his Word to penetrate into our lives in a real and practical way.

Here's That Test

Ask yourself these questions as you pray and meditate on the Word of God:

_____ Is there any area of my life that is not submitted to the Lordship of Christ? What am I doing to change this situation?

_____ What events occurred today that demonstrated to me my need to live in God's will? In which of these did the Holy Spirit speak to me the will of God for me?

_____ Am I being obedient to the will of God or am I conforming to the world that surrounds me? What am I doing about it? What does the Spirit say? What does the Word of God teach me in this regard?

———— Am I giving the Holy Spirit a chance to speak to me? Am I giving sufficient time to the Word of God, studying it and investigating it — to know the will of the Lord in my life?

———— Is there some situation in my life in which the Lord is disciplining me so that I might learn to live better under His will? How am I responding?

In your daily life, are you letting God be Who He says He is? Are you letting Him give you wisdom to live in a better way?

Remember: *The only things under the Lordship of Christ are those that you put there.*

6

I Wasn't Interested
in Making Jesus My Lord

Most of the evangelists who stayed in my boyhood home were rough, crude, poorly educated transient preachers who did not seem to want to work. That irritated my father — and convinced me even more that I didn't want to be a no-good "man of the cloth."

Preachers were lazy windbags. They didn't work — but just told other people how to live their lives. Thus, it naturally followed that religion was for people who liked to sit around and listen to these gabby ol' know-it-alls with soft hands. Church was for people who disliked to work and liked to talk too much — like gossipy old women! I wanted nothing to do with it.

However, my mother was determined that her youngest son would be a preacher — and she was quite a prayer warrior. She didn't mind sharing her concern with any Christian who would listen. She spent hundreds of hours on her knees on my behalf. I know there were times when her prayers were all that kept me alive.

For example, once, when I was eleven years old, just a tanned, skinny boy in Panama City, Florida, we lived in a house overlooking the Gulf of Mexico. I loved the ocean, as did all my grade-school buddies. One day, a bunch of us — none of us yet teenagers — built a homemade raft from scrap lumber and empty barrels. We had in mind creating a floating dock that we could haul out into the surf — out past the big waves of the breakers — so we could swim and dive from it all summer.

So, there we were, having a really good time, hammering and nailing all morning long. We were building a real wonder of jury-rigged unseaworthiness with bent-over nails, chicken wire and stomped-down pieces of splintered wood. Some time after lunch, we proudly launched our health hazard. But we had forgotten one important thing: *an anchor.*

I guess we just thought it would float wherever we dragged it — and we'd just dive and swim all summer long. We neglected to consider ocean currents and tides, which can be incredibly strong. So, we drifted out to sea. For a while, we were diving and laughing and whooping it up and not noticing that the shore was disappearing. Then somebody yelled, "Look! The tide's got us!"

Indeed, we were being dragged out by the outgoing current. In absolute horror, we peered at the disappearing shore and began yelling for help. But there was nobody on the beach to hear us.

Panicking, some of the boys started to dive in and splash toward the shore. But I yelled at them to come back. I knew that they would never make it. I could have, but I felt a responsibility to the younger ones, some of whom had started crying. Although I was scared and knew I was strong enough to get to the beach, I could not bring myself to leave my terrified little neighbors — not the first- and second-graders with their tears running down their cheeks.

"Don't leave me, Lester," quietly begged one little boy. "Don't leave me. Please don't leave me."

So, we sat on our unwieldy ship and watched the shore turn into a thin line on the horizon. As the sun began to set, the wind came up and the ocean swells began to pick up. Up we bobbed on the top of the swell, then down into the trough, surrounded by walls of water on either side. It was scary.

As our flimsy raft creaked and pitched, we hung on for dear life. I don't remember any of us praying. It wasn't our style. We were just boys, high on life, self-assured of our own immortality. We couldn't die. Only old people die — and sick people. We were neither. I was eleven years old and indestructible.

Then the ocean began to get rough. Big waves broke over us repeatedly, almost capsizing us several times. I remember ordering everybody to lie flat and hang on tight — otherwise, I knew one of the smaller guys was going to get swept off.

I watched for sharks. I hoped for a wind to push us back to land. Nothing. It seemed like an eternity as the sun hung over the western horizon, blistering our sunburned shoulders. The rhythm of the sea lulled us, but big waves kept drenching us, splattering us with cold salt spray, knocking us around and threatening our little craft.

However, suddenly, somebody yelled. One of the children pointed excitedly to the shore. "Look!" he hollered. "The houses are getting bigger again."

Indeed, the tide was coming back in! We whooped and cheered and began paddling madly.

"Listen up," I yelled, as we neared the shore. "Listen up! We can't tell *anybody* what just happened. Our parents will tan our hides."

Everybody agreed. Then the other guys dived off and splashed into the beach. I waited on the raft until everyone had made it back safely. Then I dived in and swam ashore. Man, did that sand under my feet feel great!

When I got home, my mother had a funny look on her face. "Where have you been?" she asked.

"Oh," I shrugged nonchalantly. "You wouldn't believe it if I told you."

But I had a funny feeling. I think she knew. I believe that she had been on her knees. I believe that was the only thing that saved us.

Today I cannot help but believe that as we boys were hanging on for dear life, buffeted by the big waves, my mother was on her knees.

After that, she was even more determined that I would grow up to be a man of God. She prayed for me without ceasing. Her ladies' group all prayed for me — and let me know it. She dragged me to church every time the door opened. I did not like it. I did everything to keep from listening. Sullenly, I went to every service, every Gospel meeting and every revival. I cannot tell you a single thing that was said in any of the sermons inflicted on me. But I believe some of it sank in. As a result, I was a church-going boy whether I liked it or not. That alone does something to a kid's local reputation.

Some children hung around the pool hall. Others helped the bootleggers. I could always be found at church. Why was my mother doing this to me? I much preferred the beach.

I believe much of it is because as a young girl, Mother had felt the call of God on her life to become a missionary. It was around the turn of the century and the idea of a woman missionary was not well received by her family. Even her pastor advised her to give it up. She became a housewife instead. But still she longed for her calling — and she transferred it to me. On her knees, she saw in me the missionary-evangelist that she had so longed to become.

Also, she was intent on not repeating an earlier mistake. My oldest sister, Anna, had felt an urgent call of the Lord to be a missionary to China. But Anna had disobeyed the Lord and married a non-Christian. She died early.

The heartache of what had happened to Anna weighed heavily on my mother. She was determined that I would obey the Lord's call. I was determined not to. I was ready to do whatever was necessary to avoid it. But I was at her mercy. I was the second to the youngest of seven children — Houston, Anna, Kerney, Ernest, Louise, then me and Leona. Most of them were grown up and had gone by the time I was a youngster. That made me the baby boy, which gave me something to prove.

I Had To Be a Rebel

Even as a young boy, I was hot-headed and a heartache to Mother. She dragged me to those Gospel meetings, often threatening that if I did not change my wicked ways, she was going to put me into a detention home. I remember hating those spirited, enthusiastic revival services. I refused to sing and would go to sleep on the hard benches while the people whooped and shouted and the preacher droned on and on past 11:00 P.M. Then I would be awakened and would stumble home — not to my soft bed, but to a quilt pallet on the floor, since the preacher got my bed.

I resented more and more the "holy men" snoring in my bed. I disliked them for eating my food and hogging my mother's attention. I particularly resented the fact that the visiting evangelist always seemed to rob me of my place beside my father at the dinner table. During revivals, we little children often had to eat later, after all the grown-ups had finished. It seemed to me that preachers ate and ate and ate. And they talked endlessly as they ate up all my favorite pieces of chicken. I got to wait in the shadows, wishing they would shut up, wishing they would leave, worrying that there wouldn't be anything left for me.

Revivals sometimes lasted three or four months. No wonder my dad and I disliked them so.

I disliked the preachers' goody-goody children, too.

43

Once my friend Lavert Hollifield and I took a visiting preacher's boy swimming without any of us asking permission. Winter rains had swollen the normally lazy waters of Tallahala Creek, but we were too young to know that the high water was dangerous. We stripped down to our skin and charged into the muddy current.

I swam about halfway across, but found my strength no match for the chilly, swollen stream. The current swiftly began to carry me away. As I weakened, it pulled me under.

I remember the voices. The preacher's son panicked and yelled, "Let's get home! We're in trouble! He's gone!" Then the little coward took off.

Lavert was a loyal friend, however. He dove in repeatedly and felt along the sandy creek bottom until he found me. With a desperate struggle, he dragged my body out onto the bank. I was not breathing — my lungs were filled with water. Lavert didn't know much about artificial respiration, but just turned me over and began punching my back until the mud and water gushed out and I gasped for air. He stayed there with me until my senses returned. Then together, we made it back across the creek to our clothes and home.

The preacher's kid got a whipping for leaving me. But I swore I would never have such a coward for a son. I would *never* be a preacher.

You can see I was set up. First my mother didn't get to answer her call. Then my sister Anna failed to answer hers. Now, Mother was determined that I would — whether I heard any call or not.

As I got older, I became even more rebellious. I remember stumbling home at 2:00 A.M. after one particular night of reveling with my friends and tripping over my mother's feet as I groped for my bed in the darkness.

"What are you doing in my room?" I gasped.

44

"I'm praying for you, Lester," Mother answered. Then she went down to the living room to continue. I didn't sleep easy that night. In my heart, I knew even then that God had a higher plan for my life. However, I had no intention of being a preacher. I was going to be a millionaire.

7

I Had Great Plans
To Be a Rich Man

As a little boy, I would go down to the local wholesale house and buy hundred-pound bags of peanuts. I would take them home, bake them in the oven, put them into small bags, then sell them to the men who worked at the lumber mill.

During the summer, I would build myself a wagon from scraps and cover it with canvas. Then, I would pull the wagon down to the ice house for a block of ice. Taking different flavors of syrup, an ice scraper and paper cups, I went into the snowball business. I often cleared a good profit.

So, inspired by my own abilities and the love of money, I dropped out of school at the age of sixteen. Despite my mother's tears, I went off to Mobile, Alabama, where I enrolled in barber college and became a skilled haircutter. Back at home, I was hired to operate the front chair in the main shop downtown. I loved it!

I Had a Passion for Making Money

My customers liked me — the youngest barber in town — the whiz-kid who knew all the best cuts. Then, tuberculosis struck me down. It was the scourge of my day — much as polio was during the 1950s and as AIDS-HIV virus is today. There was little that could be done about it. Rich people who caught it went off to sanitariums where they just wasted away and died. Poor people like me stayed home and waited for death.

At first, I refused to accept my death sentence. There were stories of people getting over it — just as some survived the medieval plagues of small pox and anthrax. I figured I would be one of them. But I remember getting weaker and weaker. I was too ill to work as a barber so I came home and soon did not get out of bed anymore.

My mother's ladies prayer meeting group started coming in to pray for me and lay hands on me. They were persistent, standing around the bed, pleading with the Lord to spare my life. I begged my mother to call off her prayer partners.

"Don't bring that bunch of old women back in here anymore," I kept saying. But the next week, they would be back. Under the covers, I would curse them.

Then one day, the old, white-haired doctor examined my skinny chest, shook his head and stood. I listened in horror as he quietly told my father that I probably would not last through the night.

"I'm going back to the office now," he said softly. "There's nothing more I can do. I can't even get a blood pressure reading or draw enough blood from his veins for a test."

I had been coughing up blood for weeks. Even in the night, blood would run from my mouth and onto the pillow and bed sheets. Terrible night sweats tortured me through the long nights. But that particular afternoon, I heaved up quarts of blood. I was hemorrhaging inside my diseased lungs. It was all over.

Mother stood now at the foot of my bed and wept. I could hear the doctor's solemn words to my father: "The boy is as good as dead now. Call anyone you want to see him. In two hours, there will be no life left. I'll fill out the death certificate tonight, and you come by the office to pick it up in the morning. Then you can go down to the cemetery and choose a burial plot.''

Then he left. I was seventeen years old! My time had run out before it had started. My life was over before it began. I had not had time to live — yet now it was time to die! I wasn't ready — I knew that. I was dying. And I was scared. I hung onto life.

Sometime in the dark night, I looked to the right side of my bed and there, suspended in the air was a coffin. It was bright, vivid, and very, very real to me. It was beautiful, lined with soft silk and bedecked with white lilies and red roses all around. It was turned up just a little so that I could see inside. It was empty, and I was impressed that it was just my size. But it was troubling.

I twisted away. As I did, I saw an open Bible. It was as big as my bed, larger than any book I had ever seen.

God Was Giving Me a Choice

Yes, I was being given an opportunity to obey or rebel. I could be a preacher. Or I could die. God spoke to me at that moment as I glanced feverishly from coffin to Bible and back.

"Lester, which of these will you choose tonight?" He asked. It was not an audible voice. However, it was as distinct and firm as any voice I had ever heard. God was giving me a choice. I wanted to be anything but a preacher. I despised preachers. At the same time, I was terrified at the thought of dying.

That floating coffin meant much more than just a grave. It meant hell — everlasting torment. I had heard enough preaching to know that if I died that night, hell would be my eternal destiny.

Looking straight at the Bible, I prayed, "God, if the only way in the world for me to live is to preach — then, I'll preach."

Then, to confirm what I had just said, I added. "If You will let me live as long as I preach, one day I will be the oldest man in the world, because I won't ever stop preaching."

I meant it. That commitment to preach was also my commitment to give my heart to Jesus Christ. I accepted both His calling and His full salvation. It was settled. I drifted into a sweet, deep slumber filled with a sense of destiny. My life had been pre-empted by a higher power.

When you read these words, I will have passed my eightieth birthday. Moses' life of destiny began when he was eighty years old, and he passed the sword of leadership on to Joshua at the age of 120. A man's physical age is not necessarily the determining factor in whether he holds the reins of spiritual wisdom and knowledge.

I am more than eighty years old, and I have no intention of stopping until God says it is time to stop. Yet on the other hand, part of my end-time commission is to pass on the sword of wisdom and the knowledge that I have gained and the skills God has given me to wield over the years. To whom do I pass these? To the younger generation of ministers coming on the scene.

That's why I'm writing this book to you today — *to pass the sword to you.*

8

What Are You Waiting For?

My mother did not sleep much the night I was supposed to die. She did not know about my vision of that casket and Bible. When I opened my eyes the next morning, she was standing over my bed. Her eyes were blurry from crying. But I had never seen her look more beautiful. She sensed that I was awake and asked if there was anything she could do.

"I'm hungry," I said. It was the first time I had been hungry for weeks. She turned toward the kitchen.

"I'll get you some grape juice," she said softly.

"No, what did Papa have for breakfast?" I asked. She told me that he had eaten ham and eggs, hot biscuits, grits and red-eye gravy. Well, that made me more hungry than ever.

"That's what I want!" I declared.

Mother began to cry again. "Oh, no, no, no. You haven't had anything substantial in your stomach for days. You would die!"

Remember that the doctor had gone home to prepare my death certificate anyway. Nobody had expected me to be alive that morning.

"Well," I grinned at her. "I want to die full of ham and eggs and hot biscuits and gravy — with grits."

Mother looked hesitant. "Well," she replied. "The doctor said you are going to die anyway. I'll give you your last desire."

So, she prepared the huge, hot breakfast that I had ordered. When she sat it down beside my bed, she turned her back and began to sob again. I ate. Oh, how I ate. I cleaned my plate and asked for a second helping. Mother looked doubtful, "Let's wait and see if this hurts you."

"Mother," I decided to tell her, "I am going to be a preacher."

My own mother did not believe me. She smiled bravely at me.

"No," I insisted. "Really." I told her about the vision — and my promise to the Lord.

"Oh, Lord, I thank You. I thank You. I knew You would do it!" she declared, lifting her hands in thanksgiving and praise. Her heart bubbled over. She had prayed for me as far back as I could remember. Even as a very little boy, I could remember hearing her pray, "Oh, Lord, please make Lester a preacher." Now her heart's desire had been given her.

I grew steadily stronger. Within three days, I was walking all over the house and eating everything my mother would prepare for me. In ten days, I was out fishing in the Gulf with a friend. Life returned to normal. Perhaps three weeks later, I was praying in my room and God spoke to me.

"You promised Me you would preach if I healed you," was what I heard deep within my heart. "What are you waiting for?"

With a sudden sense of urgency, I rushed downstairs to where Papa was having his breakfast.

"Papa," I declared to him. "I'm going out and preach. I'm going today."

He stared at me in absolute disbelief. He stood and began to roar in rage. Remember, Papa was not a Christian. He detested preachers.

"You're not going to do any such thing," he declared. "You're not strong enough to go. You wouldn't know anything to say if you did go."

I told him that I was plenty strong and had lots to say.

"I'm not going to have you begging for a living," he thundered. "I want you to have a real job. Why do you think I have already spent a lot of good money to teach you to be a barber?"

"Papa, I've got to go preach."

"You're not going to do it!"

"God said I had to."

"God nothing!" My 225-pound, Irish father jumped from his chair in a rage. Skinny seventeen-year-old tuberculosis survivor that I was, I just stood there trembling and weeping. I was shattered. I turned and ran back upstairs to my room.

"You'll starve to death if you do!" he bellowed after me.

In my bedroom, I fell to the floor and wept. "My heavenly Father says go and my earthly father says no," I prayed. "What can I do, Lord?"

Through my tears, God impressed upon my mind Isaiah 41:10,11. I had never read those verses, so it had to be the Lord impressing them on my mind. I pulled out my Bible and quickly found the words that I had heard in my heart:

Fear thou not; for I am with thee...

As I read that promise, I was filled with great peace. God's great love overwhelmed me. He reached down and took fear out of my being. Suddenly, I was laughing and crying at the same time. It took me about an hour to regain my composure enough to finish reading the verses:

> ...be not dismayed; for I am thy God: I will
> strengthen thee; yea, I will help thee; yea, I will
> uphold thee with the right hand of my righteousness.
>
> Behold, all they that were incensed against thee
> shall be ashamed and confounded: they shall be as
> nothing; and they that strive with thee shall perish.

"OK, Lord," I said aloud. "If You're with me, I'm ready to go."

I went to the closet and pulled out a little brown forty-nine-cent fiberboard suitcase. It didn't take long to fill it with what few clothes I had. My father had already left for work when I marched downstairs, suitcase in hand.

"Where are you going?" Mother wanted to know.

"I'm going out to preach."

"But, son, where are you going to preach? You have nowhere to go!"

"I don't know where I'm going, Mother, but I've got to go."

I kissed her good-bye and walked out onto the front porch. I would never return to that house again.

A friend of mine was out in front of the house. I told him where I was going, and he volunteered to go with me. Why not? He had nothing else to do. Together we chugged up the road in his old jalopy. We had no idea where we were going. But I was compelled by an inexplicable feeling of destiny. I was obeying. And God was going to bless it. I had made Jesus Lord of my life — even though I didn't know the terms yet. I did know that God wanted me. And I wanted Him.

I Was Determined To Obey Him

I was determined to seek God, to do whatever He wanted of me. I had a lot to learn. I had some big changes ahead of me.

As you submit to the Lordship of Christ, don't back away from the changes that you will see. Maintain a positive attitude, holding fast to that which you know to be true. Keep your eyes on Jesus!

Satan seeks constantly to subvert our emotions negatively, evoking discouragement, inconsistency, frustration and depression in us. Don't let him get away with it! Keep your eyes on Jesus! Know without a doubt that the Lordship of Christ is the best thing for your life and is the plan of God. He never plans anything harmful for us. Look to the future with hope, anticipating with joy the work of the Lord and the blessings that come with obeying Him.

Don't Let Failure Discourage You

Continue onward! Galatians 6:9 says that in time we will harvest if we do not give up. The first thing I would say to any Christian who is feeling the call into the ministry is, "You did not call yourself into your personal ministry. You have been divinely chosen and then called, anointed and sent by Jesus, the Head of the Church."

That's what Jesus said in John 15:16: **Ye have not chosen me, but I have chosen you, and ordained you, that ye should go and bring forth fruit, and that your fruit should remain: that whatsoever ye shall ask the Father in my name, he may give it you.**

Every born-again child of God has a commission and calling to take the Gospel to every creature, according to the Great Commission in Matthew 28:18-20 and Mark 16:15-18. However, it is important to know how the Holy Spirit wants you to fulfill that calling. The ministry is not another "job," but a specific calling in the Body of Christ and should never be entered into or treated lightly.

The words of Jesus in John 15:16 are very strong. *The Amplified Bible* brings out the meaning of the Greek even stronger: **You have not chosen Me, but I have chosen you — I have appointed you, I have planted you — that you might go and bear fruit and keep on bearing; that your fruit may be lasting (that it may remain, abide); so that whatever you ask the Father in My name [as presenting all that I AM] He may give it to you.**

You are a spiritual leader, but you did not call yourself. The Bible says that God set in the Church apostles, prophets, evangelists, pastors and teachers. God set them in the Church, not man.

Most ministers I know, including me, did not start their lives desiring to preach, nor did their families want them to preach. I was planning to be a millionaire by the time I was thirty! But God had other ideas for me. He wanted me to preach, so we made an agreement. I would preach if God would heal me and meet my needs. It has worked well for over sixty years, and I don't see any reason to change.

Part II
Humility Precedes Honor

9

How Can You Live
Under Christ's Lordship?

With my mother weeping, my father thundering and my little sister gawking in disbelief, I left home to be a preacher.

My friend was sitting out in front of my house in his sputtering jalopy of a car. He thought my mission sounded great. So, off we went. I can't remember whether he even told his parents. What was he doing outside my house? I don't know! Looking back, the "coincidence" of his being there and willing to go with me is downright miraculous.

Want to know something else incredible? Although I have pondered on it for thirty years, to this day, I cannot remember his name. That's right! The Lord sent a swimming and fishing friend to be a taxi driver — and revival songleader — for this seventeen-year-old preacher. I don't even remember his name, but he was there when God needed him.

Without him, would I have gotten out of town? Without him, would I have set off on foot and would my father have just come after me in our car and ordered me home? I didn't have enough money for a bus or train. I wasn't old enough to leave home. If Papa had ordered me to return, legally, I would have had to. But I had a great and glorious Father Who sent my swimming friend at just the right time and gave him enthusiasm for my wild announcement.

Sure, he wanted to go with me to be a preacher! We headed north in his old car — ready to evangelize the world. I was too naive to know that a newly converted, seventeen-year-old kid couldn't just go out and preach without any preparation. We didn't even have a church to preach in.

We nursed that old car up the road, stopping every five miles to refill the radiator. We were growing hungry, too. But we didn't have any money. We noticed a persimmon tree beside the road. It was heavy with its orange, sweet fruit. We shook the tree of its ripe bounty, then sat down in the grass underneath and ate our fill. Our faith and our spirits were high. We imagined how Elijah must have felt after being fed by the ravens by the brook Cherith.

Then, we noticed a country schoolhouse sitting out in the middle of a cotton field. Something inside me declared, "That's the place." We tracked down the farmer who owned the field and, in an authoritative voice, I announced to him: "Sir, we want to use that schoolhouse to preach in."

I remember how he looked at me with amusement. I must not have looked like much of an evangelist as I stood there in front of him in all my ninety-two pounds, my city clothes, my peach fuzz and my big Bible. He started to shake his head no.

"I've been sick of tuberculosis, and if I don't preach, I'll die," I declared to him. "God healed me to preach."

He grinned at me and didn't answer. I laid the guilt on him: "If you don't let me have that schoolhouse to preach in, then I will die, and you will be to blame."

At that, the old farmer's mouth dropped open, and the tobacco juice ran out the side, dribbling down onto his chin.

"Now, son," he drawled with a twinkle in his eye. "I wouldn't want you to die!"

"Well, let us have the schoolhouse," I insisted, not seeing anything funny. He dug in his pockets and came out with an old key. I thanked him, then under my breath, I thanked the Lord. I started to go, then thought of something.

"Would you mind loaning us a lantern, too?" I asked.

He gave it to us.

I Had My First Church Building

That night, revival began in the old country schoolhouse. I was the preacher, and my friend was the song leader. We went up and down the road, telling everybody we saw about the meeting. Eight farmers showed up the first night. Word of the revival spread. Crowds grew.

I really didn't know what I was doing. What did I preach about? I gave them my testimony! That made one sermon. The next night, I told it to them again — but with added gusto. But by the third night, the audience was restless. They didn't want to hear about my healing again. So, I had to think of something else. I told them other stories from my life, such as the close call on the raft, the time I almost drowned when the preacher's son ran off and another story about a time when I was stabbed in New Orleans.

But my sermons were somewhat lacking — particularly when I ran out of personal stories. I scrambled mentally, telling Bible stories as best as I could remember them from Sunday school. How I regretted not paying attention! It must have been the third or fourth night that the sermon flopped completely. I stared out at an unmoved, unaffected crowd and wondered what I was trying to do. I got so discouraged that I didn't even try to take an offering. I didn't give an altar call, either. My songleader, who was about to quit on me, mumbled something about going back home to his girlfriend. He didn't even lead a final song. Everybody just went home.I was dejected.

But Things Got Worse

The next morning, the farmer who had been putting me up greeted me rather gruffly at the breakfast table: "Boy, in my house, if you don't work, you don't eat."

I thought I *had* been working — preaching my heart out every night, praying and resting up during the day. Plus, none of the preachers who had freeloaded on my family for years had ever lifted a hand. They had always sat around.

"Work?" I blurted.

"Don't it say in that there Bible of yourn that if you don't work, then you don't eat?"

"Sure, but I am working. Preaching is working."

"Naw, it ain't. It's just blabbering." The farmer gestured at two big pails. "Take these slop buckets and go feed my pigs."

Do You Know What "Slop" Is?

Slop is the stuff that today we pour down our garbage disposals while scraping the dishes after meals. It's the brown leaves that you peel off a head of lettuce. It's the tops of carrots and the eggs that spoiled and the bread that molded. It's the guts of the fish and the bones of the chicken. In a farm family, the slop gathers daily in buckets in the kitchen — the spoiled milk, the rancid grease, the wormy pieces of peaches, the tough old leftover pork chop that nobody ate, and the noodle soup that went bad after sitting out all day. Nothing about slop is pleasant. It stinks — particularly after it has set in the kitchen all day and night.

The pigpen was a few hundred feet from the house. As I carried those heavy buckets, the foul stuff sloshed over onto my clothes and into my shoes and all over my preacherly pride. By the time I got down to the pen, I was upset and angry at the world and God.

I didn't even know how to call hogs. I just bellowed at them. They came. As they grunted and snorted and wallowed in their stench, tears ran down my cheeks. It wasn't fair. I wasn't the Prodigal Son anymore! I was obeying! Plus, every preacher I ever knew got to sit in the parlor and tell fine stories to all the adoring ladies. Why was I having to slop hogs? Was I being punished? Was I having to pay for my years of being a prodigal? That wasn't fair!

Throwing down the empty buckets, I ran out into the cornfield. There, I knelt in the soil.

"Lord, let me go back home. Or let me die right here. Anything, Lord, but not this!"

As I lay there, humiliated and crying, I sensed that God was trying to teach me something.

"If you will be faithful to Me in the little things, Lester, I will give you bigger things. If you won't quit, I'll let you touch many people by My power. You will yet bless multitudes."

What did that mean? *That I had to slop hogs?* That I had to change this farmer's mind about preachers being lazy blowhards?

I lay there quietly weeping as the realization began to sweep over me that God hadn't deserted me. He wasn't punishing me. He was only training me to be useful to Him.

I got up, picked up the empty buckets and returned them to the kitchen. I drew water from the well, washed out my foul-smelling clothes, took a sponge bath and began to study the Bible in earnest. I had a revival to preach. I had to learn to preach to these people. They needed Jesus.

I began to realize that I really was needed after all. And that I was going to have to work. It was important to this farmer that I get my hands dirty. Well, why not? I remembered how irked my father always was with the preachers who sat around blowing hot air, eating our food and taking up space. My dad detested the lazy windbags. So had I. Now, I was doing the same thing to this farmer who had invited me into his home. How stupid of me!

I was going to have to get some dirt under my fingernails. I was going to have to be a good example. Why? God wants us to be blameless. That means without accusation. We have to avoid doing things that cause brothers and sisters around us to stumble. Being a lazy windbag was the first thing on the list that God was not going to allow in my life. He wanted me to be blameless in the eyes of those farmers.

We Have To Be Blameless

First Thessalonians 5:23 teaches us that God desires for all of us to be kept blameless.

* In matters of the spirit, this involves cultivating a daily devotional time, an ever-deepening understanding of His will, study and meditation of the Word.

* In matters of the soul, this involves nurturing the gifts and talents that we possess, taking charge of our own minds and thoughts, transforming our negative attitudes.

* In matters of the body this involves physical exercise, abstention from destructive habits, adequate nutrition, good hygiene and proper appearance as befits children of God.

* And in matters of practicing what we preach, it means that we can't set ourselves up on a special shelf — too holy and righteous to do manual labor.

10
Manage Your Time and Your Resources!

Without knowing what I was doing, I learned how to manage my time. If I hoped to be a good witness, I had to help out with the chores. I had to pull my own weight. But I had to be prepared when I stepped into the pulpit. So, I had to use good sense. I also had to trust the Lord to give me enough time to get ready to preach.

The Word teaches that God expects us to use good sense — and to depend on Him in every decision. We are to ask Him how we should proceed. We are to seek His guidance as we manage our goods and possessions.

We all know He has commanded that a part of that which He gives to us be returned to His house. This is called the tithe in Malachi 3:8-12. Beyond the tithe, there are other ways to give for the work of the Lord. This must be made with a good attitude, according to Exodus 35:20-29; 36:2-7; 1 Chronicles 29:6-19; and 2 Corinthians 9:7.

* We must remember that giving money is not all that God requires. He expects that we will manage well all that we possess.

* We must be good stewards of monies we spend on other things, too. We cannot splurge wildly, extravagantly and intemperately, but instead must spend according to the will of the Lord. He is the master of these things, not us.

* We must be careful with that which has been given to us. We must multiply it.

The Word teaches that we are responsible for our time. (Eph. 5:15-17; Col. 4:5.) One way of learning to use our time is to establish priorities in our activities.

Consider This List

Assign a priority to each of these activities. Write "1" before the most important category, "2" before the next most important, and so on with "5" being the least important.

_____ Vocational activities (work, school)

_____ Spiritual and emotional needs of the family (family devotions, time with the children and spouse)

_____ Personal relations with God (devotions, Bible reading and Bible study)

_____ Christian ministry activities

_____ Other activities (personal grooming, watching television, shopping)

In order to better manage your time, list the activities that you must carry out. Mark with a pencil those that are essential or cannot be changed. Fill out a "Weekly Schedule" with essential activities, then add others that you wish to engage in. Ask yourself the following questions:

* Are there things that must be done that I am neglecting? What are they?

* Are there things that I am doing that are unnecessary? Can I substitute them for things that are necessary?

* Are there things that I do that can be done by somebody else? What are they?

* Can I delegate some responsibilities?

* On what things am I spending a lot of time? Are these really necessary?

11

Do You Love Your People?

That first revival lasted six weeks. During that time I baptized eighty-seven adults — dunking them out in the creek. I did a lot of farm chores, too, before the Lord blessed me and lifted that burden from me. He wanted willingness.

I Had To Be Willing To Slop the Hogs

After closing out that revival, I went thirty miles up the road and did it all again. I had learned to tell my stories with humor — and to hold altar calls with intensity and urgency. I developed a method of illustrating my sermons. I would have people from the audience put on costumes and act out Bible characters as I wove Bible stories into my sermons.

I never had any trouble drawing a crowd. I began getting invitations to minister in churches as well as schoolhouses. From one rural community to another, I worked my way up through Mississippi and into Tennessee and Arkansas, then into the boomtown oil fields of Oklahoma.

My Reputation Grew

As my reputation grew, I was called upon to do fewer chores. But I did not forget my lesson — nor did I forget why my dad had disliked lazy preachers who did nothing but talk.

More men started coming to hear the kid who didn't mind getting his hands dirty. And they came back night after night. It may have been that I was a riveting, inspiring and brilliant preacher. However, I think it had more to do with the fact that there was little else to do in the rural areas I visited. The truth is that I was the only entertainment around.

After several months, my little sister, Leona, joined me — and added quite a bit to my meetings by playing her guitar and singing. My preaching style improved steadily. It was enthusiastic, to say the least. I would jump and run and yell at sinners to repent. My voice would be hoarse, and my body drenched with sweat.

But I am ashamed to confess to you that I had the wrong motives for preaching. I didn't love these people at all. I didn't particularly care whether they went to hell or not.

No, I was preaching out of fear.

I honestly believed that if I wasn't obedient, I would die. I thought that if I gave up preaching, God would hit me with tuberculosis again, and this time it would kill me. So, I preached out of self-preservation. Yes, I was obedient. But I had not surrendered my heart.

As I talk with other preachers, I see that this sin is not all that rare. However, it is so dangerous to the spiritual health of our people.

You Must Love Your Flock

People need to feel your genuine compassion. When they gather to talk with you, they need to know that you care. When they watch you participate in the worship service, they need to know how much it matters to you that they love and praise and worship the Father. When you kneel with them at the altar, they need to experience the reality of your genuine concern and your unselfish commitment to them.

You are dealing with brand-new Christians here — and they do not know yet that they must put their eyes on Jesus. So, their eyes are on you. They look to you for wisdom, for direction and as a role model. The burden on you is awesome! As the song says, "You're the only Jesus that they ever see!" They see Jesus through you. Your attitude preaches a thousand sermons every time you shake hands with your congregation or eat dinner in their homes or visit them in the hospital.

Keep asking yourself: *If I am the only Jesus they ever see, then how would He act?* Then, remember the Jesus Who washed His disciples feet. Remember the Jesus Who spent quality time one day at the well with the despised Samaritan woman. Think of the Jesus Who had such compassion on the sick and Who loved the noisy little children who so irritated His disciples. Remember the Jesus Who declared that blessed are the humble and poor in spirit. Greatly loved by God, He declared, are they who hunger and thirst after righteousness, the pure in heart, and the meek and those who mourn. Remember the Jesus Who declared that *you* are the light of the world!

You must let that light shine so that men may see your moral excellence and your praiseworthy, noble and good deeds! Why? So they will give you a big offering? So they will put your picture on the cover of national magazines? So they will buy your books and tune into your radio show? No!

Matthew 5:17 says that we must be good examples so that others will *praise and worship our heavenly Father.* It is so ego-gratifying under the hot lights — out there in the spotlight in front of the public! You, alone, stand in all your glory, bowing to their applause, smiling in their adoration, turning and waving in the pulpit with every eye upon you. They are just waiting for some gem of divine inspiration to drip from your lips. But you must love these people —

and gently turn their eyes off you and on to Jesus Christ. How? It may take supernatural intervention. It did with me.

My motives as a young preacher were almost entirely negative. I was preaching to stay alive. I had made an agreement with God. He said that if I would preach for Him, He would heal me and let me live. I had no compassion for the people. I would preach and then tell them that they had heard the sermon and that their getting saved was their business and none of mine.

One night in mid-sermon, I asked a young woman, "Do you want to go to heaven?" She shook her head no. Almost in anger at her refusal, I told her bluntly, "Then you go to hell."

I turned around and walked back to the pulpit. I looked back and saw that she had fainted and fallen to the floor. After several ladies brought her to, I went to her and said, "You seemed healthy enough when I was back here before. What happened to you?"

"I never had anybody tell me to go to hell before," she answered, "let alone the preacher."

"Lady, there are only two places to go," I replied, "and you told me that you didn't want to go to one of them, so you're bound to go to the other."

I got a convert that night. But after preaching this way for about eighteen months, I was in a little country church in Tennessee and had an experience that would change my life and ministry forever.

I was sitting at the side of the platform while a man was leading the people in singing. Suddenly, I was no longer aware of the congregation in the church or anything around me. I saw before me all the people of the entire world. They were of every color, brightly dressed in native costumes. I was impressed with how beautiful they were as they walked down a very long and wide highway leading away from me. I saw people from every nation. I had never

70

seen a large missionary pageant before and many of the native costumes were strange to me, yet in the Spirit I was able to recognize the countries of the world they represented.

In the vision, God lifted me up until I was looking down upon that uncountable multitude of humankind. He took me far down the highway until I saw the end of the road. It ended abruptly at a precipice towering above a bottomless inferno. When the tremendous, unending processing of people came to the end of the highway, I could see them falling off into eternity. As they neared the pit and saw the fate that awaited them, I could see their desperate, vain, struggles. I watched them try to push back against the unrelenting pressure of those in the rear. The great surging river of humanity swept them ever forward. I could hear them screaming.

God opened my ears to hear the screams of damned souls sinking into hell. As the Lord brought me nearer I could see men and women of all nations plunging into that awful chasm and see their faces distorted with terror, their hands flailing wildly, clawing at the air. As I beheld in stunned silence, God spoke to me out of the chaos: "You are responsible for these who are lost."

"No, not me, Lord," I cried in self-defense. "I don't know these people. I have never been to Japan or China or India. I am not to blame!"

God's voice was tender yet firm as He spoke again: **"When I say unto the wicked, Thou shalt surely die; and thou givest him not warning, nor speakest to warn the wicked from his wicked way, to save his life; the same wicked man shall die in his iniquity; but his blood will I require at thine hand."**

That was the shortest sermon I had ever heard, and the most frightening. It was preached to me by God Himself.

Not until a week later did I discover that He had quoted a passage from the Bible — Ezekiel 3:18.

Suddenly the vision was over. I was still trembling. Opening my eyes, I saw that the meeting house was dark and I was alone there. I supposed the people had decided that I was praying in a trance and had just closed the meeting and left me. It didn't matter. A heavy burden settled down over my soul, and my heart felt like it was breaking in two. I began to weep, heaving and sobbing uncontrollably from deep inside. I prostrated myself on that wooden floor and remained there all night agonizing before the Lord.

"Oh, God, forgive me," I implored. "Forgive me for not loving the least, the last and the lost of the world."

I again made a covenant with God.

When I walked out of that little building at eight o'clock the next morning, I was a new man. Something had matured in my soul that night. I felt that I had been sanctified, set apart by God for a particular purpose. God had given me a compassion and an urgency for souls that has remained strong for over sixty years of preaching.

That night I committed to become a missionary. I knew that the charge that had been given me was worldwide. I knew it would take me to every corner of the earth, to every tribe and to every tongue and people and nation.

I renewed my fervor. But now, it was real.

12
Glorious Revival

In the next months, hundreds of souls were saved. It seemed that wherever we went, the whole countryside was stirred. After one revival, two missionaries went off to Africa. Several young men and women were called into the ministry.

But it was not always glorious.

Often the offerings were meager. I can remember one week when the total was thirty-seven cents. To top that off, I heard people complaining that I was overpaid since I didn't have to pay anything for room and board. Well, let me tell you, living in strangers' homes is no treat. I would gladly have paid for a hotel.

Once in the little town of Charleston, Arkansas, we had morning and evening services, but response was very light. A few women came to the 10:00 A.M. meetings, but at night, it was bad. It was hot. The only "movement" seemed to be the constant waving of the hand-held cardboard fans provided by the local funeral home.

Although attendance was light in the mornings, the ladies all had a sweet spirit, and their prayers were filled with a genuine hunger for revival. One morning, I said to that little group, "I feel led to pray for those of you who have not yet received the Holy Spirit."

As I began to pray, I laid my hand on the nearest lady. She was immediately filled with the Holy Spirit. She reached over and touched the next lady, who also received the Holy Ghost and then reached over and laid her hand on the woman next to her. In domino fashion, five women were filled with the Spirit in not much more time than it takes to snap your fingers. I sensed that the heavenly breezes were blowing — that revival was on its way.

Then a woman who had not been attending asked to speak to me. She shared that she had been impressed to stay at home to fast and pray for our meetings and for true revival to result. She told me that she had been fasting and praying for ten days when God gave her a vision. She said that while she was at home praying, she saw the blood of Jesus dripping from the cross and falling right over the church door. In the vision, she saw people trying to dodge the blood as they entered the church, but that all who were touched by blood were cleansed from sin — and that their lives were changed.

Well, that very day it began to rain — both literally and spiritually. We had a thunderstorm that I was certain would keep everybody home. I showed up soaking wet with the crease out of my trousers and the starch out of my shirt. To my absolute amazement, however, the church was packed. The song service was powerful. I preached under heavy anointing — and the altar was filled. Testimonies resounded from the rafters.

One of the most sober and conservative businessmen in the community was suddenly convicted in the middle of a baptismal service down at the creek — and waded right into the water in his suit, tie, shoes, watch, billfold and all.

A woman testified that while she had been doing her laundry, she had been prompted to look up — and had a vision of heaven. She jumped and cried as she described the beauty and splendor of New Jerusalem. Her description was so real that she caused everyone to want to go that heavenly city!

There was a dramatic show of supernatural power, too — which stunned us all. A young ruffian who had been standing outside the church with his rowdy buddies suddenly noticed that his sister had responded to the altar call. This young man actually burst into our service and pushed his way to the front. Grabbing his sister, he pulled her up from her knees, threw her across his shoulder like a feed sack, then carried her outside. There, in front of his drunken friends, he scolded the humiliated girl and ordered her never to go back to church.

A few days later, this young man was plowing a field behind his house. The sun was shining, but a tiny black thundercloud formed in the sky. From that little cloud came a bolt of lightning, striking him dead and setting his clothing on fire while his parents watched from the farmhouse window. You can imagine the town's reaction to that event. His drunken friends were at the altar that very night.

After several weeks of wonderful moves of the Spirit, the time came to close the revival so I could travel on to another appointment. However, as my sister and I were packing the car, a large crowd gathered and begged us to stay. They lay down on the car and wept, crying out, "You can't leave town yet. We have loved ones who aren't saved yet and are going to hell."

Well, we unpacked the car and the revival continued for another week. I had learned to love these people.

But, you may be saying, "Lester, how could a seventeen-year-old kid just go out and announce that he was a preacher? Didn't you need some credentials? Didn't you need papers from some denomination?"

Frankly, it did not occur to me. Remember that it was the 1930s, the country was not completely through with the romance and violence of the Wild West, and had just been plunged into the Great Depression. Times were different. Churches were not so institutionalized and traditionalized.

Nevertheless, after several months, I did decide that I needed some sort of credentials. I needed to belong to some church group and submit to their authority. I didn't realize that it was unnecessary. God had already ordained me. But I jumped at the chance when a preacher in Arkansas offered to let me be in an ordination ceremony with several other young ministers. I stood up with about forty other men and the general superintendent of that association came by, patted us all on the head and said, "You are ordained."

About an hour later I saw the general superintendent outside.

"Brother, God bless you," I said.

"Who are you?" he asked.

"I'm one of the those you ordained an hour ago."

"Oh," he replied, "you are?" and walked away. I was very disappointed. A teenage boy doesn't know much, but I knew that was wrong. My feelings were hurt. The man who had ordained me an hour before didn't know me or anything about me.

Today, I realize that formal ordination should come from the local church where you have grown up spiritually. They will know if God has already ordained you. They know you and love you and care for you. They will help nurture your ministry. The local church knows your strengths and weaknesses, and can encourage you in the rough times.

Jesus, the Head of the Church, does the selecting, and God's Holy Ghost does the true ordaining and anointing.

Men should not attach exalted titles to themselves. I tell people to just call me Brother Sumrall. I'm sure I'm a brother. I'm not sure of anything else. I'm even uncomfortable with the title Reverend. That title comes from the word "revere," which means to venerate, honor and adore. There's nothing about me that should be venerated or revered. No, I want my people to get their eyes off me and on to Jesus! He alone is worthy!

The Apostle Paul scolded people who bowed down to him and worshipped him. The angels who appeared to men in the Bible invariably told them to get up and not to worship them. Only God is to be adored and revered. Certainly not me. Indeed, we are given several warnings about letting people adore us.

Look at what happened to Herod the King in Acts 12:22,23. He gave a beautiful speech, prompting the people to declare: **...It is the voice of a god, and not a man** (v. 22). In the next verse, remember, the angel of the Lord **...smote him, because he gave not God the glory: and he was eaten of worms, and gave up the ghost.** That is not something I want!

But we live in an age of pride when men want to lift themselves up. Some think that if they put the word "prophet" before their name, it will make them a prophet. If you are a prophet, you are the same as a banana tree. It doesn't need a sign saying, "I am a banana tree!" It just bears bananas. If you are something great in the Kingdom, you don't have to wear a sign. The fruit will come, and when it comes, everyone will know who you are.

The devil would like for all of us to be proud, and we must not allow pride to deceive us. Any gift that we have comes from Jesus. He should get all the glory. We do not need to exalt ourselves. The Lord will promote whom He pleases.

Everybody Is Ordained!

In John 15:16 Jesus said that He chose us and ordained us to go! Every one called by God should be ready to *go!* God never saved any of us to sit still.

Go!

Begin with your family. Go to your friends. Talk to the people you work with. Christianity is a going thing. When it doesn't go, it dies. Don't wait for everything to be "right" before you go.

The happiest preachers in the world are those who don't have to say, "See my fruit?" No, God sees it. He sees the converts — the ones they have led to Jesus. There's no greater joy for a preacher than to bring forth much fruit. I have fruit all over the world — people who are going to heaven with me, and who look to me now as their father in the faith.

Jesus said that those He chose would go and bring forth fruit, and that their fruit would last. He also said that the fruit should remain. You and I have to protect our fruit with our prayers.

Through all my years of ministry, my fruit has remained and is strong today because I command it to remain. I started on the mission field when I was twenty, establishing new churches. Most of them remain strong and vital today. Those who prophesied that my work would die are very embarrassed, because it remains. I believe what Jesus said in John 15:16. I claim that promise in prayer. I tell my fruit to remain, and command the devil to leave it alone, and my fruit does remain.

Jesus made a promise in this verse. He said that when He chooses and ordains us to go and bear fruit that remains, He will provide everything we need to get the job done, so that whatsoever we ask the Father in His name will be given to us.

You and I have a source, and it's not man. If we are bearing lasting fruit, God will be our Source. I've proved Him over and over for more than sixty years in all parts of the world, in every kind of condition and environment. Jesus promised me when I started out that if I would give my life to preaching for Him, He would take care of me. He has taken good care of me for over sixty years. If I need a new shirt, I just ask the Father, and He gives it to me.

Usually two! I have some beautiful, expensive shoes a pastor in Africa gave me. He said that God told him to buy me a pair of shoes. He didn't even know what size, but the Holy Spirit told him, and they fit perfectly.

I Pass the Sword to You

How can you know that you are called and ordained and anointed? Perhaps the best way to answer that question for yourself is to recall how Jesus knew He was called and anointed. Luke recounts that Jesus read Isaiah's words:

> **The Spirit of the Lord is upon me, because he hath anointed me to preach the gospel to the poor; he hath sent me to heal the brokenhearted, to preach deliverance to the captives, and recovering of sight to the blind, to set at liberty them that are bruised,**
>
> **To preach the acceptable year of the Lord.**
> **Luke 4:18,19**

When Jesus read those words, He knew that the Spirit of the Lord was applying them to Himself. In fact, He stated in verse 21 to those who heard Him: ...**This day is this scripture fulfilled in your ears.** When you can face a congregation, read the above quotation from Isaiah that Jesus read, and say to the congregation, ''This day is this Scripture fulfilled in your ears,'' you will know that you are called and anointed.

13

God Will Take Care of You
— Even Against Assassins

I was preaching in the Oklahoma oil fields one night when suddenly there was a squeal of tires and a sickening thud. Someone outside began to yell, "A man has been killed!"

I heard another voice say that a drunk had staggered out in front of a speeding automobile. Well, I took advantage of the dramatic situation and gave a strong altar call, pointing out that this man had been drunk and had given his life to the devil — and now he was dead and in hell. Passionately, I invited sinners to give their lives to Jesus. As the wail of sirens filled the air, the prayer rail was packed to capacity.

However, the next morning, a car pulled up in front of the house where I was staying. Three or four sullen young men piled out, banged on the door and demanded to speak to me. No sooner had I stepped out onto the porch than one of them shoved me and another informed me: "We are going to kill you."

"What for?" I stammered.

"Our daddy got killed last night, and he wasn't drunk."

"Oh, I'm so sorry," I apologized. "I'm glad he wasn't drunk. I didn't mean any personal offense."

"Well, offense is taken," bellowed another one of the boys. "You preached a whole sermon against our dead daddy. You called him the town drunk. You said he's burning in hell. Well, you'd better watch your back, because we're going to send you there to join him.''

As the boys backed out of the yard, one of them pointed a finger at me a last time. ''We're going to get you,'' he threatened. Then, with a squeal of rubber, they sped away.

I was shaken. I went to my knees, asking the Lord to forgive me. I asked for His protection, His guidance.

I arrived at the meeting an hour early and was surprised to find that about a hundred people had gathered to see what was going to happen. I heard somebody ask the local pastor, ''What are we going to do?''

''I'm going home,'' he answered, not looking at me. ''Somebody is going to get killed here tonight.'' And he left.

It was still fifteen minutes before time for the meeting to start, and the people were obviously scared. Some of them began to come up to me and express concern. ''What are you going to do?'' they asked, their faces filled with worry.

''What do you mean?'' I asked.

''Son,'' said a deacon, ''those boys are coming to kill you tonight. You talked against their dead father. They have vowed to shoot you dead tonight if you step into that pulpit.''

''In that case,'' I answered, ''let them kill me. They told me they were going to send me to the devil. Well, they can't. I belong to Jesus. If He wants me to join Him in heaven tonight, I'm ready to go.''

With that, I got up and started a song, led in prayer and jumped right into my sermon. But people were scared. They had come to see blood. Repeatedly, I was warned by some that my life was at risk and that I needed to step down from the pulpit.

"Listen, God is with me!" I finally shouted. "Anybody here who pulls a trigger against me will die. God Himself will strike him dead. I dare you to do it. Quit stalling around. If you're going to do it, stand up right now and do it."

As I spoke, the fear of the Lord came upon that place. The audience sat open-mouthed in stunned silence. I finished my sermon and opened the altar. Several people responded. However, I stared at a grim-faced young man sitting in the crowd. I called out to him from the altar. "Young man, God is talking to you tonight!" I declared to him.

"How do you know?" he rebutted, standing.

"God tells me that He is talking to you."

"Don't you know who I am?" he asked.

"No, I don't, but God does," I responded.

"It was my daddy you were talking against," he shouted. "I have come here to kill you."

And with that, he pulled out a gun. I had not recognized him until that moment.

"Listen," I told him, "I don't know where your daddy is, but I know you are going to hell if you don't get right with God."

He never did point the revolver at me. Instead, he broke and began to weep bitterly. I led him down to the altar and as he knelt, he was joined by dozens of his oil field friends. What a glorious night! Our God reigned! Many were saved.

Daniel's prophecy was clear, **...but the people that do know their God shall be strong, and do exploits** (Dan. 11:32). If you want to be strong and do exploits — such as staring down an assassin — you must know your God. To try to do exploits for God without knowing God in an intimate, personal and powerful way is to follow the example of the sons of Sceva. They attempted to cast out evil spirits without a personal and powerful relationship with God. The demons overpowered them, and they had to flee for their lives. (Acts 19:14-16.)

To have power in the Spirit, we must continually build ourselves up in the Spirit. When we pray in tongues, our spirits pray, and we build ourselves up in the spirit, according to 1 Corinthians 14:2-4. In spite of "...**scoffers who...**" **follow mere natural instincts and do not have the Spirit....build yourselves up in your most holy faith and pray in the Holy Spirit,** declares Jude 18-20 (NIV). Praying in the Spirit, praying in other tongues, must become as much a part of you as the beating of your heart.

But I have another confession for you. At that time, I was not filled with the Spirit. I was operating mostly in my own strength. The Lord used me, but I was so empty. And I knew it.

14

God Does Not Accept Commands

Although I had been raised among Pentecostals, I had not experienced the Baptism of the Holy Spirit. I knew that I was the recipient of our heavenly Father's outpoured forgiveness and love. Romans 8:1 became real in my life: **There is therefore now no condemnation to them which are in Christ Jesus, who walk not after the flesh, but after the Spirit.**

But, something was missing.

I Wanted To Be Filled With the Spirit

Although my reputation as a fiery young teenage evangelist spread, I was weighed down by a feeling of emptiness. I wanted to have the Spirit living within me. I was well acquainted with this doctrine of the Baptism of the Holy Spirit through what I had seen all those years of being dragged to my mother's church. But this gift had not fallen on me. Desperately, I sought it.

One of the first sounds I ever remembered hearing was that of my godly mother speaking in an unknown tongue as the Spirit gave her utterance. Having been reared around Full-Gospel folks all my life, I thought that receiving the Holy Spirit would be no problem. But it became a personal heartache.

Why Did God Choose Not To Bless Me?

Often, I would preach about the Holy Spirit. But it was not from my own experience, just from what I had heard and seen, as well as what I had read in the Bible. I admonished others that they should seek the blessing. Many of them did — and received it. This caused no little controversy. People would say, "This boy has no right to preach about the Holy Ghost. He doesn't even have the Baptism himself."

They were right. But I was completely open about my lack — which brought me even more criticism. I would tell the congregation that they should seek the infilling, then I would join them at the altar seeking it myself. Yes, this was a little odd.

When other people had received the Holy Spirit after my altar calls, sometimes folks would gather around me and pray that I would receive the Baptism. I can remember so many times that they tried to "pray the preacher through." They would lay their hands on me and instruct me to repeat nonsense syllables or the words "Hallelujah" or "Glory, glory, glory."

In my heart, I rebelled against that method. I didn't want to fake anything. Nor did I want the Holy Spirit to come as a result of working myself into a frenzy. I felt that it should be supernatural — from Almighty God.

After I had been preaching about a year and a half, I was in Dyersburg, Tennessee, where one of my older brothers lived. I was preaching at a little white frame country schoolhouse outside town. My brother didn't want to come, but he sent his wife to listen to my preaching and give her opinion of my ability as a preacher.

When we returned, I was in my room, and I could hear voices through the fresh-air vent. I heard my brother ask his wife, "Baby Doll, how did Lester do?"

Back through that vent, loud and clear, I heard her say, "Bud, Lester wouldn't make it if he preached a thousand years!"

A thousand years? I didn't have a thousand years! I began to weep and cry before the Lord. I had just started preaching. I was still a teenager, and my relatives said I would never make it. So I cried out to God about what a hard time I was having and now about what my own brother was saying. I thought that maybe it was time to quit.

As I lay on the floor, hurting all over and crying out to God, He spoke to me again.

"No!" He said. "You can't quit! Would you read Luke 4:18,19?"

I didn't know what it was, so I opened my Bible and read the words of Jesus:

> **The Spirit of the Lord is upon me, because he hath anointed me to preach the gospel to the poor; he hath sent me to heal the brokenhearted, to preach deliverance to the captives, and recovering of sight to the blind, to set at liberty them that are bruised,**
>
> **To preach the acceptable year of the Lord.**

I knew those verses applied to me because Jesus lives in me. I looked at that passage and said, "Lord, do you mean that?"

"Yes, I do," He said. "My Spirit is upon you, and when people meet you, they will know you are a person that My Spirit is upon."

"Really?" I asked.

"Yes," He answered. "You're not always going to be out here in country schoolhouses. You're in training now. My Spirit is upon you, and I have anointed you!"

Isn't that amazing? God's Spirit was upon me, and He had anointed and ordained me to preach the Gospel to the poor. The Lord told me that He was anointing me to preach the Gospel to people who had never heard of Him before, people who didn't know Him — people who were down and out and had no friends, people who were poor in spirit with nothing in their souls.

I studied the passage carefully. I knew I was finding more direction for my life. But, still, I wanted His infilling. I believed that I was supposed to manifest the Holy Spirit's presence within me by sudden and dramatic speaking in tongues.

Yet, Nothing Happened

One night, after ten people had been saved and filled with the Holy Spirit in my meeting, I came home dejected. I had been down at the altar seeking the Baptism with the rest of them. But I didn't receive anything.

I went back to the room where I was staying and lay down on my bed disgusted. As I stared up at the bedroom ceiling, I mumbled aloud to myself, "Here I talk about this, and I don't have it. What's wrong with me?"

God began to deal with me: "You have felt that you could just grab anything you wanted when and how you wanted it," He spoke into my heart.

He was right. I had decided that you got the Holy Spirit by pushing the right buttons. I felt that if you followed the formula, God was forced to reward you. It doesn't work that way.

God Is Not Bullied

God does not take orders.

Sure, He was honored when I fasted and prayed for the infilling of the Holy Spirit. But, He did not like my attitude. I had tried to earn the Holy Spirit.

Well, God did not want me preaching such heresy. So, He taught me this lesson in a dramatic way. He let me go down the biblical check list, do everything right, then demand my blessing. And He did nothing. He was not going to let a smart aleck teenager who thought he had all the answers go uncorrected. He waited until He had my attention. He had humiliated me in front of scores of churches by giving old men, pretty girls, farmwives, car mechanics and would-be assassins the gift of the Holy Spirit. And I got nothing but divine silence.

So, now that He had my attention, the Lord told me simply: "Since you didn't receive the Holy Ghost your way, now I am going to give the Spirit to you as a free gift."

Suddenly, the glory of the Lord came into that room as I had never felt it before. The Spirit of the Lord seemed to flow from the corner of the room until it touched the foot of my bed, my feet and came up through me. As it did, I began to speak in a heavenly language I had never learned.

God had filled me by his grace — and had demonstrated to me that I should never, never preach that His blessings can be conjured up through our efforts. I have seen so many fall away from the Lord when they ordered Him to cure their loved one or bless them with riches. They were disappointed because He does not take orders.

The next morning, I announced to the folks where I was staying, "I received a blessing last night."

They all glanced around knowingly. "Everybody knows it," said the farmwife quietly.

Hmmmm, I wondered. I hope I didn't keep everybody up all night.

Nothing more was said. I really don't know whether I disturbed their sleep — or if the glory of the Lord was miraculously manifested to them individually, too, or what. But I launched into my joyous calling with renewed vigor. I had always been a strong athletic competitor. In school I had boxed, wrestled, played football, basketball and baseball, and had run track. I played rough. I played to win. And I loved it. Now I threw myself into my preaching with the same enthusiastic abandon.

My mission field was the Deep South of the Great Depression. People still carried firearms and lynched horse thieves. I'd had a rowdy, enthusiastic life before my conversion, and now I preached according to the man I was and the disposition God had given me.

15

I'm Not Promising You
a Rose Garden

Christian ministry was not easy then — nor is it easy today. It is no bed of roses.

Today, so many churches are a mess.

Recently, I talked with a friend who lamented that great revival was about to break out in his church, but that such a move of the Spirit was irritating the deacons. They, he said, were all members of a fraternal organization and had decided among themselves that church was supposed to be a nice, traditional place to come on Sundays — not an emotional, enthusiastic hotbed of proselytizing.

All this talk of evangelism was downright irksome to them. Why would the church want to have a Vacation Bible School for other people's children? Why should the church pay for a speaker to come in for a special outreach seminar? After all, if the church grew any more, who was going to pay for a new sanctuary? In the deacons' opinion, the preacher was just stirring up trouble.

''I don't even feel like this is my church anymore because of you,'' one of them told the preacher. ''I don't know most of these people in the pews. Do any of them give? Why should we have a nice church building for them?''

Pathetic!

However, attitudes like that are more common than we like to admit. But you cannot let it get you down. You can't just quit — anymore than I could when the Lord did not fill me with His Spirit or when I heard my sister-in-law report to my brother that I would never make it as a preacher in a thousand years.

You Have To Fight!

At the end of his life, the Apostle Paul wrote to Timothy that he had fought a good fight and had kept the faith. From the time he saw Jesus on the Damascus road until Nero took off his head, Paul fought a good fight and never quit. Here's what he wrote about himself:

> **For I am already being poured out like a drink offering, and the time has come for my departure. I have fought the good fight, I have finished the race, I have kept the faith. Now there is in store for me the crown of righteousness, which the Lord, the righteous Judge, will award to me on that day — and not only to me, but also to all who have longed for his appearing.**
>
> **2 Timothy 4:6-8 NIV**

Paul was so successful because he refused to quit. Whether he was facing persecution from the civil authorities, natural disasters, flak from the Jews, betrayal from false brethren or struggles with personal sin and weakness, he refused to quit.

One of the most important pieces of advice I can give to a young preacher is, don't quit! When you understand that God is the One Who appointed and anointed you, and that He equips and empowers you for the job, then you realize that the only way the enemy can get to you is to throw obstacles in the path to discourage and dishearten you to cause you to quit.

I have had many opportunities to quit over the last sixty years. Several times I wanted to give up and get out.

When I announced I was going to preach, my father immediately tried to discourage me, telling me that I would starve to death. He told me I couldn't preach and that nobody would want to hear me anyway. I knew what God had told me, but a seventeen-year-old boy still puts a lot of faith in his father. When my father told me that he wouldn't help me and that I would starve in a few weeks, it made me want to quit. But I remembered the vision, and I remembered that God had healed me while the doctor was writing out my death certificate. I had promised to preach.

So I Did Not Quit!

As far as my father and the world were concerned, I was starting out into the Great Depression with no money and no hope of survival. But God gave me a promise, found in Isaiah 41:10,11:

> **Fear thou not; for I am with thee: be not dismayed; for I am thy God: I will strengthen thee; yea, I will help thee; yea, I will uphold thee with the right hand of my righteousness.**
>
> **Behold, all they that were incensed against thee shall be ashamed and confounded: they shall be as nothing; and they that strive with thee shall perish.**

I left home believing that God was God, that He had spoken to me and sent me out, and that everything would work out all right. I remember almost quitting once when the entire offering after a week of preaching had been twenty-six pennies. My father had told me that no one would want to hear me preach and that I would starve to death. When I thought about what he said and got twenty-six cents for a week's work, I was tempted to doubt that I had heard from God.

But I didn't quit.

I know a preacher who said that he would give up and quit preaching. He was pastoring a thousand people, driving a new Lincoln and had a top salary. But he said he was quitting because the first two or three years were real hard and he didn't believe God had taken care of him. I told him I didn't understand. I asked him if he thought a boy could leave home to become a carpenter and expect to get paid the first day the same as a master carpenter. He said he did not. So I asked him what right he had to expect to have the same things as some grand old man of the faith the day he got out of Bible school.

You have to grow in God, and grow in maturity, and never quit. When Abraham left Ur of the Chaldees, he didn't have near what he had at the end of his life. He just believed what God told him and refused to quit.

When that old farmer wanted me to slop his hogs, I almost gave up. I could have quit right there. It was a perfect opportunity. Who wants to feed dirty, smelly old hogs? I felt that I was trying to serve God and being treated like the Prodigal Son. I was weeping before God, and He spoke to me and said, "If you won't quit, I'll bless you!"

"Lord, do you mean that?" I asked.

"If you won't quit here," He answered, "I'll bless you further there."

"Lord, I'm willing," I responded. I got up and fed the hogs. I don't know how long I had to work around that farm — it was several weeks — but God kept His promise. I obeyed and refused to quit, and although I had to work and help out many times, I never had to feed hogs again.

I'm glad I didn't quit when my life was threatened, because when you quit you go backwards. Quitters never go forward. If they do start again, it's at the end of the line. But I did learn to be more cautious and wise about what I said about people or situations, and to make certain that I knew what I was talking about.

In later years when I went around the world preaching, I was in many difficult places facing dangers and hardships

I never dreamed of. But I could face them and come through safely and victoriously because I had the promises of God and the commission of the Holy Spirit. I knew that I hadn't chosen this life but that God had chosen me and equipped me.

If I had given up and quit in those early days when friends and family and circumstances were against me, I would never have known the promises and provisions of God or the joy of bearing fruit for the Kingdom and seeing that fruit remain and grow. The opportunity to succeed carries with it the opportunity to fail. The opportunity to win carries with it the opportunity to lose. The opportunity to fulfill your calling carries with it the opportunity to quit.

When faced with an opportunity to quit, remember your calling, and these words of an anonymous poet:

Go on, go on, go on, go on,

Go on, go on, go on,

Go on, go on, go on, go on,

Go on, go on, go on!

You cannot quit. No matter how bad things are in the world. No matter how bad things are in the churches!

These are grim times in so many places worldwide. My heart goes out to those who write to me of their terrible hardship — on every level imaginable. In some countries such as Argentina, inflation has reached such unimaginable levels that prices in the supermarkets are raised three times a day. In the drought-parched sand dunes of Chad and the typhoon-ravaged tidal islands of Bangladesh, however, there are no supermarkets. And in Russia and the Ukraine and Byelorussia, the supermarkets are empty.

In America, I hear from longtime partners in my ministry who are feeling very real physical, financial and emotional pain as well. They are unable to find work and are being torn apart by worry as they watch their finances disappear. Some tell of losing their businesses and their homes. They ask for prayer as they struggle to hold their families together. They share dismaying doctors' reports. They tell of being cheated by people they thought were friends. They report losing everything in investment collapses.

I hear from parents whose children are into the occult and sexual sin — at such incredibly early ages. I hear from teachers who are frightened. I hear from people who are wondering if prayer can really make a difference anymore. Theirs is very real and overwhelming pain. It is devastating.

I have to tell you that the despair of millions is terrible and very real. The spiritual darkness in some of our big cities is oppressive. There are sections of New York City and Los Angeles that the police have written off as too dangerous to enter.

God Wants You

But I have one answer: God wants *you*.

No matter how difficult things seem to us, God is not limited by economic downturns or crop failures or dwindling resources. The same power that parted the Red Sea and fed the five thousand — and raised Jesus from the dead — is available to us, His children, when we lift our needs to Him in prayer.

I believe you have felt a call on your life to serve God in a mighty way. I don't know what God has called you to do — whether to preach or teach or clip the church lawn. But I can tell you that we need a zealous new generation to take up the sword of truth and continue the assault against the gates of hell!

Our Battle Has Many Fronts

Today evil people claiming to be Christians are signaling the end of time by gaining disciples with bogus and easy gospels!

I'm not just talking about such obvious false teachers as the popular non-Christian cults. No, I am talking about people who move among us, pretending to be great Christian leaders, but living lives that are an absolute shame in the eyes of God. These people are causing terrible disgrace to the cause of Christ as they defame our loving Father.

I'm not just talking about the televangelists who have been denounced on the TV evening news. I'm also talking about preachers who no longer require that their followers turn from sin. Ministers who do not denounce laziness and wickedness and disobedience in their midst.

I am talking about Bible teachers who shirk from mentioning the Lordship of Jesus Christ or the New Testament's required submission to Him. Instead, motivated by greed and a lust for power, these preachers set themselves up in high places, exploiting simple people with a counterfeit gospel that strokes egos, endorses mediocrity, claims to boost ''self-esteem'' or ''recovery'' or ''personhood'' — but really just wanders off after any popular human message of the day.

Such people are ear-ticklers. They have sold out. Some have just given up — tired of being fired by deacons and church boards who dislike preachers who rock the boat. Others are completely corrupted by the power that religion offers them — and will tell their flock anything to gain personal power and get hold of money.

In their covetousness, these leaders have sunk so low that they regard their followers as a source of profit. In their lust, they exploit believers. Some fleece the flock with a feel-good, entertaining gospel that does not require anyone to change, is without a real, personal Jesus and takes advantage of the human lust for an easy way to heavenly reward and earthly prosperity.

Others seem to crave power and popular acclaim.

Faced with all this, I can only shake my head in disbelief. It can all sound so good. But there is only one Gospel.

16
Ministry Is Not Easy

I want you to understand that nothing about being a preacher or teacher or evangelist is going to be easy.

In the second chapter of 2 Timothy Paul has some great advice for his young disciple. He clearly warns Timothy not to get involved in foolish arguments that only upset people. Instead, he points out that God's servant must not quarrel, but must be gentle and courteous to everyone.

We must not resent injuries to our reputations or insults to our personal pride. We must be patient teachers, gently correcting those who are on the wrong path. We must respect our elders and intercede for those who are in danger of being led astray. We must pray that God will give them a change of mind, a repentant heart and a personal realization of the truth — so they can come to their senses before they are seduced in their minds and hearts by Satan to do his evil will.

In the third chapter of this letter Paul also warns Timothy that in the last days it is going to be particularly hard to be a Christian because of the wickedness that will prevail. He prophesies that in the last days people will become selfish, self-centered and greedy. They will be lovers of money, boastful, haughty, abusive. They will be mercenary, blasphemous and given to bitter words. They will have no respect for their elders, no gratitude, no interest in praising God. They will be lacking in love for their brothers, unable to make up after arguments, never forgiving an enemy, eager to spread scandal and rumor.

They will have no self-control or any desire to do good. Instead, they will be hostile to the righteous, brutal, unfaithful — eager to betray their friends. They will love pleasure more than they love God — lusting after sensual pleasures and vain amusements rather than worshipping their Creator.

Here is the scary part. They will maintain a facade of religion, an outward form of holiness — a bogus Christianity which denies and perverts the true message of the mighty power of God.

The last days are upon us, my friend. Some of our worst headaches will take place in churches where we would expect to be enveloped in the love of our fellow believers.

There are some hard times ahead for you and me.

But We Will Have Peace in the Storm

God never leads His people out into the wilderness to die. He will protect us.

You will have to depend on Him. You will have to seek Him urgently and daily. He will provide. He will guide. He will be there. Even when unfaithful deacons and gossiping ladies' Bible studies groups do everything possible to defame you. Even when the piano player accuses you unfairly of making advances.

Worse Than Gossip Is Pride

One of the saddest things I see in the Church today, including the ministry, is a spirit of pride that wants to isolate Christians and Church leaders and keep them away from hurting people. It is too easy to get comfortable in our jobs, and hide behind the pulpit or administrative responsibilities and not be willing to get our hands dirty with the work of the Gospel ministering to hurting people.

The magnitude of pride cannot be fathomed. Look at Lucifer. He was not only an archangel, but the anointed cherub that covered the throne of God. (Ezek. 28:14.) God called him the Son of the Morning, the "light bearer." God said that he was perfect in beauty and full of wisdom.

As God has created all intelligent beings with a power and authority of decision making, this beautiful creature heard himself speak marvelous words, observed the Shekinah glory of the Trinity flowing through him, measured the vast wisdom put within him, and decided in self-exaltation to attempt to place himself above the throne of God. This attitude caused an insurrection in heaven, and Satan, along with one-third of the angels was cast out. (Is. 14:12-15.)

Pride is one of the chief enemies of the destiny of all mankind. When you conceive in your mind that you do not need God for life's decisions, and think you should have more appreciation from others and be exalted above others, you have lost that vital relationship of humility that is born of the Spirit of God.

What a tragic situation for one who knew humility to end up in pride and have to be removed by God.

God is so sensitive to this type of thing that when Moses — who had talked face to face with God — disobeyed and struck the rock, saying, "Shall I bring forth water?" God told him that he would never set foot in the Promised Land to which he was leading the people. (Num. 20:7-12.)

In my experience over the years, I am amazed at those who began humble and were destroyed by pride. I remember meeting that remarkable man in Great Britain, Stephen Jeffries, and witnessed some of the most impressive miracles of healing in this century through his ministry. But when he stood up before thousands of people and said, "The world is at my feet," within a year he was crippled with rheumatoid arthritis. It was a horrible disease he had seen hundreds healed of, but from which he died because of his pride.

Please receive from me the spiritual covering of humility and do not exalt yourself. Your gifts and importance are for the Kingdom of God and not to be wasted on your own life.

Pride Can Destroy You

I remember when I was a young man starting out preaching. I was one of the speakers at a conference. A woman came to me after my sermon and told me that I was the greatest preacher she had ever heard, and she knew because she had heard them all. I was only about nineteen then, and my head really swelled. Here was a woman who had heard every preacher around for years, and I was the greatest.

The next night a friend of mine was the preacher, and after the service I watched the same woman walk up to him and tell him exactly what she had told me the night before. She said that he was the greatest preacher she had ever heard, and she had heard them all.

My feelings were hurt, and my ego was crushed. But God spoke to me that night and told me to learn a lesson from that incident. The Spirit of God said to me, ''Other people's heads are not the place for your happiness.''

Never form your opinion of yourself from what any person says. It matters not what people think and say. People's opinions will change with the wind. The important thing is what God says about you. Always go by the Word of God and the Spirit of God speaking to your heart. People will flatter and lie, but God will always tell you the truth.

Don't be proud. Be humble. Let very common people talk to you. God may be speaking through them, and who knows? They could be great someday.

The Bible says that we should not think of ourselves more highly than we ought. (Rom. 12:3.) It is amazing how many preachers get caught up in pride and material gain.

Be a humble person. If you are humble, people can see it in your eyes, and they can hear it from your mouth. Your whole being will speak it. You don't have to say anything.

If you pastor a large church, or your ministry begins to grow, the money will start to come in, and the temptation will arise to hoard it and spend it on your own lusts and pleasures. Then the devil will take advantage of that situation, and you will come to love money more than souls. Stay humble and free from greed. Use the money that comes in to feed the hungry and preach the Gospel, and God will trust you with more.

Paul Admonished Good Conduct

Paul wrote to young men whom he had trained, admonishing them on how to conduct themselves. Paul told Timothy: "Don't let anyone look down on you because of your youth." I know, as Paul did, that young men are important and need to be nurtured.

You need to know your purpose and how to conduct yourself. Paul told Timothy to let no one despise him because he was young, and that the way he would be respected was to be a good example. (1 Tim. 4:12.) He gave Timothy a list of five ways to be an example, covering all aspects of life.

Guard Your Mouth

First, Timothy was to be an example in speech.

The most powerful weapon you have is right under your nose. It's called your mouth. You can use words to bless people and get the lost saved and delivered, or you can use words to murmur, complain and stir up strife and give an opening for the devil to work in your life.

James says that the tongue is an unruly evil, full of deadly poison, that no man can tame. (James 3:8.) With it we bless and curse. (v. 10.) No man can tame the tongue, says James, but the Holy Spirit can. Any child of God, and especially a minister, should guard his tongue from speaking evil against his fellowman or murmuring against God. James admonishes us to . . . **be swift to hear, slow to speak, slow to wrath** (James 1:19).

Guard Your Actions

The second thing Paul admonished Timothy to be was an example in his conduct.

You are in a fish bowl when you start preaching. People watch your every move. Some do it from bad motives, wanting to catch a minister in some sin or impropriety. Others set men on a pedestal and try to pattern their lives after them. Some just look to a minister as a spiritual leader, one whom they should expect to trust for godly counsel and example.

Whether the motives are good or evil, the fact remains that you will be watched, and your conduct should never bring reproach on the Church. I have seen men have affairs with women in their church, or divorce their spouse and marry someone else, then come up with some hogwash to justify it. That is not right. You are to be an example in your conduct.

Walk in Love

Third, Paul tells Timothy to be an example in love.

The New Testament is full of references to love. Jesus said it was the new commandment. (John 13:34.) John says that if you love your brother you abide in the light, and there is no cause for stumbling in you. (1 John 2:9.) If you love your brother you won't be constantly arguing, feuding and splitting churches over doctrinal arguments or money.

When I was on the mission field, I would leave everything except my clothing and personal items to the local church or the next missionary coming in. When I built a church, I would immediately turn it over to the local Christians.

Remember, it is God Who called you and promised to take care of you. Don't be taking your brother in Christ to court. Better to let God give it back to you a hundred fold. Be an example in love.

Love will build friendships that last. Friends are your greatest treasure, more than money and material goods which rust and perish. So build friends. Trust people, and you will be happy.

Faith Is the Victory

Next Paul admonishes Timothy to be an example in faith.

The greatest example of faith in my lifetime was Smith Wigglesworth, a simple, uneducated plumber who shook the world with his faith. The secret to his great faith came in his relationship to God. He lived in the Word, eating it with every meal. The Word of God and the Spirit of God were closer and more real to him than any person on earth.

Keep Yourself Pure

Finally, Paul exhorts Timothy to be an example in purity.

Satan has unleashed a spirit of immorality on the world as never before in history. The "sexual revolution" of the sixties was only the beginning, to soften up people for what is now going on and will continue.

Immorality is rampant in our society, including the Church. It has become such an open problem that I devoted an entire book, *Overcoming Compulsive Desires*, to thoroughly discuss the problem. In this chapter I will only mention two major reasons why I believe men fall into immorality.

The first situation that may cause a minister to fall into adultery is a lack of caution when counseling someone of the opposite sex. A person coming for counseling, especially for marital problems, is usually in an emotionally wrought state, often feeling hurt and rejection by her spouse and needing to feel loved and appreciated.

Another reason men fall into immorality is a failure to guard their minds. We are responsible for what goes into our minds. What the world is putting out on television, in movies and in many books and magazines is filth from hell. Men of God have no business reading pornography or watching seductive movies or television programs. I have had dirty books given me by preachers who laugh and say, "You'll enjoy this." When someone gives me something with filth in it, I don't read it, and I don't leave it for someone else to get. I destroy it.

Never Travel Alone

I make it a point never to travel alone. Nobody ever has to say, "Where is Lester Sumrall?" Everyone knows where I am. When I leave home, my office has the telephone number where I am staying. I can always be reached. Whenever possible I take my wife with me.

You should either be home with your family or out preaching the Gospel, surrounded by people who will protect you and build you up spiritually. Don't allow yourself to be found in questionable places with the wrong people. Keep your guard up and refuse to give any place to the devil.

Refuse To Fantasize

Don't fantasize with evil or worthless thoughts in your mind. Paul admonished the Philippians to think on things that are true, honest, just, pure, lovely and of good report — things that are virtuous and praiseworthy. (Phil. 4:8.)

''What can I do when I hear the devil whispering evil thoughts in my ear?'' you ask.

Scream, ''*Go!*'' and it's already a mile away.

Paul told the Galatians to walk in the Spirit, and they would not have trouble with the flesh. (Gal. 5:16.) Stay busy doing spiritual things. Some people do nothing and leave their minds open for demonic attack. Don't waste your time. If you were around me, you would find me working all the time, writing books or preparing sermons. If I wake up in the night and can't go back to sleep, I don't lie there and fantasize. I get up and start writing, or spend time in prayer or meditation in the Word.

You must guard your mind. *You* must do it.

The devil will work through the desires of your flesh and the filth of the world to pull you into immorality and uncleanness. You, individual minister of God, must personally take a stand and refuse to participate in any form of uncleanness.

Paul wrote to the Romans: **Neither yield ye your members as instruments of unrighteousness unto sin: but yield yourselves unto God...**(Rom. 6:13.) He put the responsibility on our backs. It is a matter of what we watch, what we listen to and what we yield our members to. We have the blood of Jesus to cleanse us from all sin, the Word of God to instruct us, the Holy Spirit living in us to help us overcome evil and the grace of God to pull us through any temptation. We have no excuse for falling into sin.

But if you do sin, confess it and let the blood of Jesus cleanse you. Don't let guilt and pride keep you away from Jesus. Run to Him and get free. Ask the Holy Spirit to help you overcome temptation when it comes.

Part III
God Will Take Care of You

17

God Will Take Care
of Your Daily Needs

December 19, 1931, was the night I received my vision of the millions dying worldwide without Jesus — the vision I have already described in which the Lord showed me that I was responsible to take His Gospel to the nations.

That same night, far away in London, England, the general superintendent of the British Assemblies of God, Howard Carter, was praying. The Holy Spirit began speaking, and the message so moved him that he wrote it down:

"I have found a companion for thee: I have called a worker to stand beside thee. He hath heard my call, he respondeth, and he joineth thee in the work to which I have called thee.

"I have called him, although thou hast not seen him. He is called and chosen and shall join thee. Behold, he cometh — he cometh from afar. He cometh to help thee to carry thy burden and be a strength at thy side, and thou shalt find pleasure in his service at thy side, and thou shalt delight in his fellowship.

"He shall come at the time appointed and shall not tarry. At a time thou thinkest not shall he appear, even when thou art engaged in My work."

What did this Word from God mean?

The next morning, Carter read it at a staff meeting of the Hampstead Bible Institute where he was president.

"Oh, you are going to get married," said one professor. "God is going to bring you a pretty woman from some far country."

Carter shook his head. No, the message said *"he* cometh," *"he* cometh from afar," *"he* cometh to help thee." The prophecy didn't say anything about a woman. Carter knew that God was going to send a man to travel with him.

Eighteen months passed. Each day, Carter expected the promised helper to arrive. Then, he received an invitation to speak at a camp meeting in Eureka Springs, Arkansas, in the United States.

At first, he declined — feeling it was a waste of time to travel so far for such a short meeting. He wrote his regrets, then received a transatlantic cablegram from Arkansas, asking if he was coming. Apparently his letter had not yet arrived. The wording of the cablegram moved him. He cabled back, "Ignore letter, am accepting." His missionary secretary in London suggested that he should extend his trip to visit the missionaries in the Far East before returning home.

Feeling that the missionaries needed to be visited, Carter decided to seek divine guidance in the matter. Locking himself in a local church sanctuary for several hours, he sought the Lord's will. In his solitude, he felt God speaking to him:

"Go thou for the journey and clothe thee for the path which thou shalt take, for I am sending thee, and I will go with thee. Thou hast waited for Me, and thou hast done well, for thy waiting has been thy wisdom, and thou hast been shown the path and I will give thee grace to tread it. Thou shalt speak My words and shalt follow My leading and do My will."

The message went on to assure Carter that it was God sending him out and not any human — and that his task was to go to the nations "where My servants labor. Thou shalt comfort My people and cheer those who have labored for Me. In dark places shalt thou give them help, for I am with thee.''

And so, Carter set off for Arkansas.

Meanwhile, I was preaching in Oklahoma. I often recalled my vision and grew restless as I waited for God to open the door for me to fulfill it. I wanted to get to the nations so badly that I didn't know what to do. I would preach to Americans and see Chinese in the audience. Other times, the crowd would appear to be Africans or Japanese. I would stand before the people with tears running down my cheeks because I was crying for the heathen. But no missions board was willing to send out an unproven, teenage evangelist with no Bible college training.

I was preaching a revival in the oil fields when I heard that a great British evangelist was going to come to the Tri-State Camp Meeting. In my prayer time, the Lord impressed me to close out my revival and go to the meeting in Arkansas. When I went to the church that night, the pastor did not confirm my word from God. Angrily, he told me that I had an obligation to stay and finish the revival.

''That's just the trouble with you new young preachers,'' he lashed out at me. ''You don't have any respect for your elders. You don't do what you're told. You promised to be here, and you should be here.''

I told him that I really wanted to finish the revival, but I was compelled to go. He never did understand.

My sister Leona and I drove to Eureka Springs the next morning — arriving just in time to hear Carter lecturing on the gifts of the Spirit. I had never heard anyone teach on the gifts before that morning and was absolutely amazed at what I heard.

It was while Carter was in prison for being a conscientious objector during World War I that God had revealed to him the phenomenal truth of the gifts of the Holy Spirit. Today the Charismatic world follows his teachings on the gifts.

Following the service, I met Howard Carter on the sidewalk outside. I shook his hand and thanked him for bringing the Word of God. Then I heard myself saying: "Wherever you go, I will go. Over the highest mountains, over the tempestuous waves of the sea, into the deep valleys, into the plains." I did not understand what this meant. I stopped and apologized to him.

"I'm sorry, sir. I don't usually talk like that to people."

He smiled at me and said, "Come with me to my hotel room, and I will tell you why you have spoken as you have."

When we reached Carter's hotel room, he took out a small black book of prophesies from his suitcase. He opened it and shared with me that the words I had spoken were the very words God had given to him in London many months earlier. Then he looked straight at me and said, "You are the one!"

After Carter and I talked, we agreed to travel the world and pursue a worldwide missionary venture together. It was glorious!

My dreams were being realized!

I drove Leona back home to my parents' house — but suddenly en route I realized that Carter had not given me an address where he could be reached in California. I had no idea where he was. Nevertheless, I sold my car, secured a passport, then headed to California. I was certain he was going to Los Angeles. Or was it San Francisco?

18
God Will Guide You

I went to Los Angeles. That great city during the 1930s was nothing like it is today.

Listen, if you are looking for a mission field, consider Los Angeles! Some people think that New York City is the war zone of American cities. Well, Los Angeles is also beset with terrible woes. The streets are awash in the blood of children murdered in spiraling gang warfare. The police are under constant attack — both physical and verbal. I do not envy them their job.

But back in the 1930s, Los Angeles was enough to intimidate a small-town boy who had just spent several years preaching among farmers and oil field workers. It looked mighty big. As I got off the train, I looked around.

I did not see Carter anywhere.

Should I have? He did not know I was coming. I had no idea where he was. But I really did expect to find him quickly and easily. I pulled out of my pocket a piece of paper that had the name of a large church, Bethel Temple. Upon arriving at this enormous church, I asked for the pastor and was introduced.

"I'm Lester Sumrall, an evangelist," I said in my high, Southern, teenage drawl.

"Yes, I know," Dr. Turnbull replied with a smile. "Howard Carter spoke about you. He said you would preach here for me."

"Where is he?" I asked hopefully.

"I think he's in Japan," he answered.

Japan?

He had left without me!

I was baffled, but not completely discouraged. Then, later in the day, I was told by another minister that he was sure Carter had already gone on to China.

China?

Then, somebody else disagreed and advised me that I should look for him in India.

India?

I was stunned. But I felt I was supposed to continue — to join him. My meager savings were dwindling. I had just enough for passage to one of those countries. But which one?

Where was I supposed to go?

Japan? China? India?

In my room, I was very unsettled. I spoke absolutely no Japanese, Chinese or Hindi. Plus, I would be spending every cent I had on my fare. I would be landing in a foreign country with about twelve dollars in my pocket — and absolutely no idea where to look for Howard Carter.

I got down on my knees. Was this whole thing a mistake — a wild goose chase? Should I go home and tell my father that he was right? Maybe I ought to go back to being a barber. I knew the answer even before I prayed: No, I was to continue.

"But, Lord," I prayed, "I don't know where Howard Carter is! What shall I do?"

I felt a strong impression from the Lord to buy a ticket to the bottom of the world and work my way up. What?

Where was the bottom of the world? Antarctica? No, I felt in my spirit: *Australia.*

Australia?

At least they spoke English there. But how would I find Howard Carter in Australia? And why hadn't he told anybody in Los Angeles that he was headed for Australia? Was I really hearing from God — or was I hearing my own imagination? What should I do?

What else could I do? I set sail for Australia.

One of the ministers, three times my age, drove me to the pier and inquired into my finances. I had twelve dollars, but since Howard Carter and I had agreed to travel entirely by faith in the provision of God, I considered it none of this preacher's affair.

"But, my dear young man," the brother said, "you will starve."

"Then will you please send a small tombstone," I replied, "and have it inscribed, 'Here lies Lester Sumrall — starved to death trusting Jesus'!"

While I spoke my faith boldly to him, I was still unsettled by what he said. He was a minister three times my age with much more wisdom and experience than I. My mind was telling me again that it was time to quit, but I knew what God had promised me, and I remembered the covenant I had made with Him. So I refused to quit, believing I could trust God to meet my every need. Before I saw Carter again I was to learn how to listen to God.

I Am So Glad I Did Not Quit

Just recently, I heard of a pastor who refused to quit in one of those little churches that sprang up after one of my revivals in northern Arkansas. I remember vividly how that church started.

The little town was a little more ''Wild West'' than some. In the middle of one of my sermons, a man came in and accused another man of adultery. They both pulled guns and bullets flew. One of them fell dead — I forget which one. The other took off before the sheriff arrived.

Well, I gave an altar call like no other. With that dead man lying there in the aisle, with the people gasping in shock, I proclaimed that it was time to turn or burn!

''Look at him!'' I proclaimed, pointing to the dead man. ''It's too late for him. But it's not for you!''

As I remember, most of the audience came down to the altar. That corpse in the aisle was the most effective object lesson any preacher could ever want!

Well, in the last fifty years, that little church has been a beacon of light in that community. Sure, it has had its ups and downs. In recent months, it was making a real impact in its little Ozark community — which is still a little rowdy. The main industry is an enormous chicken processing plant that uses a lot of unskilled labor. Those people work hard and live hard.

Well, this little church has had a fantastic Saturday morning children's outreach — mostly reaching out to the chicken plant workers' unchurched children. It was a mighty ministry. They were busing in children from twenty miles away. Lives were being changed! The Sunday morning service was dynamite, too! The praises and songs of God's people resounded into heaven. And the preacher was so anointed! That man denounced sin! He demanded change in people's lives! He led charge after charge against the gates of hell.

Then Satan found a way to fight back. One woman accused the pastor of wearing too-tight pants to play tennis. I'm not joking. She had no proof, but she was a very effective gossip. She had a grudge against him, too, since he had convicted her to quit gossiping. She disliked his message. Her pride was wounded. So, she spread it all over town that he was a hypocrite for wearing skin-tight, too-revealing pants when he was playing tennis. She got the deacons of that little church to fire their young firebrand.

When the congregation rose up in protest, the new members learned that they could not vote in the congregational meeting because they had not been members for a full year. So, the firing was upheld by the old-timers, some of whom had been unsettled by all the changes in their church.

Well, God is protecting that outreach to all those children. It continues uninterrupted. He has protected that preacher. It turned out that the deacons had forgotten that they had given him a contract — and that since they could not prove that he had done anything wrong, they owed him $8,000! They had to pay him! That young preacher was deluged with offers from other churches. He is going to be just fine.

His Source Is the Lord

No weapon formed against him will prosper.

Nor is the ministry destroyed. The church continues to be one of the most powerful forces in this little mountain community. All the other little churches in town have gotten new members from the blow-up. Some are wounded and wary. But they were taught to love Jesus. They are seeing that, indeed, all things do work together for the good of those who love the Lord!

My friend, such adventures are in store for you if you are going into the ministry. God wants you, but He does not promise you Easy Street. It's going to be a challenge. With His help, you will rise to the challenge — and there is such urgency! We've got very little time left. The battle is turning far more vicious than any of us expected.

However, Satan cannot *really* do us any harm. *Not in the long run.* Not in the general scheme of things.

The forces of darkness have handed us an entire generation that cannot tell the difference between right and wrong, that has been trained to give into its lusts, and which knows almost nothing about Jesus Christ — except the regrettable message that televangelists are fakes, conspiring to steal retirees' life savings.

But guess what? This empty, hurting generation is so desperate for answers. Sure, they are listening to the New Agers. They are inviting door-to-door representatives of cult religions into their living rooms. But they are open to you and me, too. And we have the only real Answer.

God is calling missionaries to New York City and Russia and Harvard University! He is calling men and women to start home fellowships — reaching out to the many who are soured on "organized religion" — but who yearn for communion with their heavenly Father and want to hear the message of ordinary people in whose daily lives Jesus Christ is real.

The Islamic world beckons — seemingly impenetrable and immune to traditional evangelism. But God loves them, too! God loves Moslems and is heartbroken when even the most blood-thirsty terrorist or the most gentle Saudi Arabian bureaucrat dies without Jesus Christ. Our Lord is grieved when anyone dies without any hope of salvation!

God is calling young men and women to start storefront evangelistic outreaches on Hollywood's Rodeo Drive and in Buenos Aires's Colon Boulevard and in Houston's barrios! He is summoning ministers who will take the Gospel back into the biggest and most powerful churches — and suffer the terrible indignities afforded anybody who stands up for truth and the Gospel rather than sectarian politics and compromise.

God is calling earnest spiritual warriors who are willing to sacrifice everything. Everything.

He Will Provide for You

God will give you the finances you need. The Bible teaches that the plan and wish of God is that His children prosper materially and live in health. (3 John 2.) In His Word, God instructs His children in the principles of justice so that we can enjoy His blessing and provision. We must always remember what the Bible says concerning the material goods of the children of God. They are His. We are only the stewards.

What was Abraham's material condition after he obeyed God in Genesis 13:2? Abraham did not have a passion to be rich. This is demonstrated in his obedience to leave everything — his land, his relatives and the house of his father — when God ordered it. He set off for an unseen Promised Land in obedience. (Gen. 12:1.) Abraham was not a person who got rich at the expense of others, instead he left such concerns in God's hands. For his obedience, God prospered him.

God's plan for blessing His children empowers us to live a lifestyle distinct from that lived by people tied to this world. We must live with both hands open: one hand open to receive, the other to give. We must be channels of God's blessing.

How wonderful if through our obedience, we can cause others to glorify Christ! Let us be the light of the earth, set on a hill! Let them see the benefits of His love through the blessings awarded to those who love the Lord. Let us not be embarrassed to express our faith in His provision — and our confidence in God's protection. Let us be happy givers, blessed by our giving, glorifying God and being richer toward Him.

Is it required of the Christian to tithe? It was right for our ancestors Abraham and Jacob before the coming of the Law. So, if Abraham and Jacob tithed and prospered, should we not tithe as well?

We do not say this merely to justify our beliefs in tithing. Abraham's and Jacob's lives prove that God honors His promises — and from our blessings today should flow undeniable proof of His goodness! Let us make up our minds to glorify God with this lifestyle, being generous, full of faith in His Word, giving with our eyes on the Lord. It does not matter if others defraud us; our reward always comes from our heavenly Father. Conformed to His promises, we will reap what we sow. God has vowed that those who live His way will not lack any good thing. (Ps. 84:11.)

19

Jacob the Schemer

Young ministers today can learn by the examples of God's chosen men and women of the past.

Jacob is an outstanding example of a man chosen by God for His purposes in the earth. But Jacob, knowing his calling, refused to wait on God, but instead lived a life of trickery and deceit until God finally confronted him and transformed him.

The problem started at Jacob's birth, when he grabbed his brother Esau's heel as they were coming out of the womb. The name "Jacob" means one who overreaches or supplants. God had told Jacob's mother, Rebekah, that the older son would serve the younger, even before they were born:

> **And the Lord said unto her, Two nations are in thy womb, and two manner of people shall be separated from thy bowels; and the one people shall be stronger than the other people; and the elder shall serve the younger.**
>
> **Genesis 25:23**

Because he was the first to come out of the womb, Esau was heir to the birthright. Under the patriarchal system, the birthright was a spiritual authority that placed the eldest son in the position of prophet-priest to the family upon the death of the father. It also entitled the eldest son to a double portion of the father's property.

Esau was the heir to the birthright by natural means, but God said that He had chosen Jacob, and would give it to him. But Jacob was a scheming, headstrong youth who teamed up with his mother to cheat and lie to get what God had promised to give him freely.

Esau came in from the field one day faint with hunger. Jacob seized the opportunity and offered him food in exchange for his birthright, which Esau agreed to. The Holy Spirit, in Hebrews 12:16, called Esau a profane person for selling his birthright. In our society we may not understand the significance of what Esau did, but God saw that he disdained the things of God, counting them of no more importance than one meal, so God rejected him as the heir of promise.

Though God had chosen Jacob, and Esau had proved his contempt for his spiritual heritage and given up his right, Jacob still thought he had to lie and manipulate to get what God had promised him. When Isaac was old and going blind, Jacob and his mother, thinking that Isaac would soon die, conspired together to trick Isaac into giving the blessing to Jacob over Esau. (Gen. 27.)

When Esau learned that Jacob had stolen the blessing due him, he became bitter and disliked Jacob, and vowed to kill him as soon as their father was dead. Rebekah overheard and told Jacob to flee to his uncle Laban's home in Syria. Because of Jacob's rash act, enmity developed between the brothers which lasted for generations and plagued the Israelites years later when they returned to the land.

When Jacob went to his uncle Laban's home, he met a man more shifty and underhanded than he was. Laban tricked him into marrying the wrong woman, and got him to work for him for twenty years for his wives and livestock. Still God's promises were with Jacob, and he multiplied his livestock over Laban's. When Jacob finally left Laban, he had worked twenty years and Laban had changed his wages ten times. The Bible tells us in Galatians 6:7: **Be not**

deceived; God is not mocked: for whatsoever a man soweth, that shall he also reap. Jacob thought he could succeed by trickery and human calculation, but as we saw before, had he waited, God would have freely given him the things he conspired to get.

After Jacob left Laban and started back toward Canaan, Esau came out to meet him. Jacob was frightened, certain that Esau was planning to kill him and his family. Once again, he refused to trust God, but devised another scheme, sending his family out in groups, thinking that if Esau did attack, some of them could escape. In desperation, Jacob cried out to God, still not understanding how to trust the Jehovah God of his father, Abraham: **Deliver me, I pray thee, from the hand of my brother, from the hand of Esau: for I fear him, lest he will come and smite me, and the mother with the children** (Gen. 32:11).

God Transformed Jacob's Life

That night Jacob met an angel and wrestled with him until dawn. When the angel tried to quit, Jacob refused to let him go until he had received a blessing. The angel told him that his name was changed to Israel, a prince with God, because he had wrestled with God and prevailed. (Gen. 32:24-28.)

The name "Israel" means God rules. Jacob had finally overcome the name Supplanter and had received a new nature through the power of God that would eventually manifest itself in a changed life.

The angel touched Jacob's hip and threw it out of joint, and Jacob carried this reminder of God's chastening the rest of his life. (Gen. 32:29-32.) God transformed Jacob from a selfish, deceiving, manipulating, headstrong young man to a servant concerned for people, and changed his name from Jacob, the Supplanter, to Israel, "God rules." This happened at a point of desperation for Jacob, when he finally cried out to God to deliver him, after all his efforts had failed.

The greatest blessing God has promised to you in your ministry will always be just beyond your grasp, as long as you strive for it. As it was with Jacob, your struggling and grasping will only delay His anointing and greatest blessing. It was after Jacob had his inward nature changed that the greatest blessings of the Lord came upon him.

If you are building your ministry, God isn't. If you are ruling your life, God isn't. And if God isn't prospering you in ministry and ruling your life, the problem is in you.

Do you really want to receive the sword that is being offered to you? Then prevail in prayer with God until your inner nature is totally under His control. You must "let God arise" (Ps. 68:1) in your life before He can scatter the enemies who come against you. Only as you let Him arise in your life is your relationship with Him such that He will entrust you with His sword.

20

Joseph's Three Coats Plus One

Now Israel loved Joseph more than all his children, because he was the son of his old age: and he made him a coat of many colours.

And when his brethren saw that their father loved him more than all his brethren, they hated him, and could not speak peaceably unto him.

Genesis 37:3,4

Joseph was called and anointed by God for a very specific and important task that would affect his family, the world he lived in and his father's descendants for generations to come.

When Joseph was only seventeen, God began to reveal His plan for his life in a series of dreams, where Joseph saw first his brothers, then his brothers and father bowing down to him. The first mistake Joseph made was to run immediately and tell his brothers about his dream. They already disliked him because he was his father's favorite son. That was Jacob's mistake. Parents should never show favoritism to one child over another. It will breed jealousy and discontent, just as it did in Joseph's case.

1 The Coat of Sentimentality

Jacob was so obvious in his favoritism that he made a special coat of many colors for Joseph. God does not like that. I call it the coat of human sentiment.

One day, Jacob sent Joseph to find his brothers where they were tending sheep. They saw him coming with his special coat, and jealousy overtook them. They plotted to get rid of this dreamer. (Gen. 37:18-20.)

At Reuben's intervention they did not kill him, but sold him to some Ishmaelite traders who took him to Egypt. The brothers then took the coat of many colors and dipped it in animal blood so their father would believe that a wild beast had killed Joseph. Jacob's favoritism and sentimentality had brought him to grief over the son of his old age whom he thought he would never see again. (Gen. 37:20-28.)

Joseph found himself in Egypt on the auction block as a slave. He could have become discouraged and bitter toward God at this point, blaming the Lord for this calamity, but he didn't. He remembered the dreams of his youth and knew that the day would still come when his father and his brothers would bow down to him.

2 The Coat of Human Authority

Just when all seemed lost and hopeless, Joseph was bought by Potiphar, the chief of staff of Pharaoh's army. What did Joseph do? He learned the language of Egypt and soon rose, by the grace of God, to the position of chief servant in Potiphar's house. Because Joseph served God in integrity, Potiphar learned that he could trust him. Potiphar gave Joseph his second coat, the coat of human authority. (Gen. 39:1-6.)

Nothing in the world can hold you down if you trust God, walk in integrity and work hard. I remember when God called me to the Philippines. Starting a new work was hard work. Then, I had made a bold move which seemed strange to many. With only a small group and a directive from God to start a church, we purchased a B-52 airplane hanger and erected it on a downtown lot that had been cleared by a World War II bomb.

However, we ran into difficulty with the mayor's office. The Lord moved in a dramatic way. It was an experience that would shake the Philippines and be the key to a massive revival. Manila would never be the same again.

One evening, I was listening to the news when through the radio came a series of piercing screams followed by pandemonium.

"Help me! Help me! They are killing me!" a young female voice cried out. Then I heard the girl scream again. Such a haunting, tormenting scream it was — the scream of one possessed by demons. I had dealt with demon-possessed people before, and I recognized those screams.

The radio announcer explained that they were in Bilibid Prison where a young girl named Clarita Villanueva had been picked up in the streets of Manila for vagrancy. She claimed that she was being attacked by demons and displayed several bite marks all over her body. I fell to the floor and began to weep before the Lord for that little human being who was being tormented so savagely. I continued praying, asking the Lord to cast out the demons and deliver her.

Early the next morning, God impressed upon my heart that I was to go to the city jail, and He would use me to deliver the girl. Because I was a foreigner, I had to take certain precautions and respect certain protocol. I couldn't just walk into the jail and set the girl free. It took most of a day to secure permission to minister to her.

That first day I was only able to meet her. When Clarita first saw me, her eyes widened and she snarled at me and hissed, "I don't like you." I recognized that was Satan speaking through her lips. As I returned to my home that night a holy anointing came upon me, and I entered into the greatest spiritual battle of my life.

127

After a day of prayer and fasting, I returned to the prison. I was angry with Satan and rebuked him in the name of Jesus. As I commanded the demons to come out, they seemed to realize it was their last struggle. They cursed and screamed, but suddenly Clarita relaxed, and I felt she was released. The glazed look left her eyes. She smiled, and an indescribable peace enveloped all of us. I asked Clarita if the demons were gone, and she weakly replied, ''Yes.''

Through an interpreter I explained to her what had happened. I told her that she needed to pray, to request forgiveness of her sins and to ask Jesus to come into her heart and receive Him as Savior and Lord. I showed her from the Bible that the blood of Jesus had cleansed her, but that the demons might make an attempt to return, and if they did she must resist them in the name of Jesus. (For a complete description of Clarita Villanueva's deliverance, see my book *Exorcism.*) Several years later, I met the Christian man who married Clarita. He told me that they were still active in church and that their children all loved the Lord.

God used this dramatic deliverance to open up the city of Manila to our ministry. People began to understand that there was more to religion than church services, pomp, parades and gaudy garments. The permits for our building that had been held up in the mayor's office were cleared in ten minutes, and the mayor became a personal friend of mine. He arranged for us to use the famous Sunken Gardens of Roxas Park for one month of revival services.

More than thirty thousand people came every night and more than 150,000 made decisions to trust Jesus as Lord and Savior. Bethel Temple became the largest Christian church in the city and mothered churches in Quezon City, Naic, Pasig and Caloocan, plus Bible classes, outreach stations and preaching centers elsewhere.

At the height of the revival, the Holy Spirit began to deal with me about leaving the Philippines. Within the next two weeks I received a cable from the pastor of the church in South Bend, Indiana, saying, "I am leaving next Sunday. The people have no pastor. Do what you wish about it."

As I read the cable, tears came to my eyes. I knew what God wanted me to do, but I was reluctant to leave the revival at its height. Many told me that the revival would fizzle out if I were not there. But once again, I listened to the Holy Spirit, trusting Him to finish what He had started.

The church we established in Manila grew to be one of the largest and strongest in Asia and remains strong to this day, in spite of all the prophesies to the contrary.

So, I left the Philippines to return to South Bend. I had given my life to missions all over the world, leaving all my possessions behind at each mission station. I returned home at fifty years old, and I didn't even own a folding chair. My friends told me I was finished. I may have looked finished, but God had other ideas. He spoke to me then and said, "I am ready to bless you." God has blessed our ministry with television stations, a worldwide radio network, a beautiful new church, a Bible college and a Christian school.

Often when we think it is the end, God is only beginning. Jesus can take you when you are a nobody and bless you and use you if you keep the right spirit, love and care for people and stay humble before God.

Potiphar's wife falsely accused Joseph, and he was put in prison. Once again Joseph found himself in the pit facing possible death, where he could have given up and blamed God for his plight. But the real strength of Joseph's character was his refusal to give up on God, even in the worst of circumstances. (Gen. 39:7-20.)

In prison, just as in Potiphar's house, Joseph became the model prisoner. Soon he had the trust and respect of the jailer as divine favor followed him:

...But while Joseph was there in the prison, the
Lord was with him; he showed him kindness and
granted him favor in the eyes of the prison warden.
So the warden put Joseph in charge of all those held
in the prison, and he was made responsible for all that
was done there. The warden paid no attention to
anything under Joseph's care, because the Lord was
with Joseph and gave him success in whatever he did.
Genesis 39:20-23 NIV

3 The Coat of Divine Revelation

It was in prison that Joseph would receive his third and
final coat, given by God this time. It was the coat of divine
revelation, and he would never lose this one.

Pharaoh had put his chief butler and chief baker in the
same prison, and while there both dreamed strange dreams.
God gave the interpretation to Joseph. The baker would be
killed in three days, and the butler would be restored. It
happened as Joseph said, and as the butler was returning
to the palace, Joseph asked him to remember him before
Pharaoh. (Gen. 40:1-14.)

Needless to say, the butler did not remember Joseph.
He was, no doubt, so happy to be back in the palace that
he put all thoughts of prison out of his mind for good.
Meanwhile, Joseph was in one of the greatest tests of his
life. Remember, he was still a very young man, in his mid-
twenties. He had already been betrayed by his brothers and
sold as a slave. He had worked his way up to be the
supervisor of Potiphar's house, only to be betrayed again.
It looked as if the dream would never come to pass, but
Joseph refused to give up on God and His promises.

It was two years later that Pharaoh had his strange and
troubling dreams about the seven lean cattle eating the seven
fat cattle. He called all his magicians and wise men to the
palace, but no one could tell him what the dream meant.
Then the butler remembered Joseph, languishing away in

the king's prison. Immediately after Joseph interpreted Pharaoh's dreams, he was made prime minister, second in command to Pharaoh himself, with unlimited power in the land to prepare for the years of famine. (Gen. 41:1-39.)

Joseph was thirty years old when he became prime minister. (Gen. 41:46.) Thirty seems to be a year of destiny for many in the Bible. Jesus was thirty when He began His ministry. David was thirty when he became king. Thirty is often an important landmark in a person's life.

Most people's lives are divided into three stages. As we saw before, the first thirty years we are receiving. From age thirty to sixty we are using, and when we get to age sixty we start giving it away. That is the sharing period of life. I will share more about this later.

Here Joseph stood before the most powerful ruler in the world of his day and told him to find someone wise and discreet and place him over the land to take up a fifth of the harvest in the good years so they would be ready for the years of famine. (Gen. 41:33-36.)

Pharaoh looked around and decided that there wasn't anyone wiser or more discreet in the land of Egypt, so he gave the job to Joseph — made him prime minister on the spot! Now that's what you call instant success — out of a jail cell and into the office of prime minister the same day! God had given Joseph his third coat, the coat of divine authority, and he would live to be 110 years old and never lose this one.

God can put you wherever you need to be to do the job He has called you to, if you will humble yourself before Him and trust Him completely, no matter what the circumstances look like. Give God the glory, and He will exalt you to the place you need to be.

Just as God had said through Joseph, the world had seven plenteous years followed by seven years of famine so terrible that no one remembered the good years. The people brought their money, then their land, then finally sold themselves into servitude to Pharaoh to get food to eat. (Gen. 41:53-56.)

The famine affected the entire world, including Joseph's father and brethren in the land of Canaan. Jacob heard that there was food in Egypt and sent his sons with money to buy grain for the family. When Joseph's brethren arrived in Egypt, they were taken into the presence of Joseph, but they did not recognize him. Joseph was seventeen years old when he was sold into slavery, and now he was thirty. He had an Egyptian name and spoke the Egyptian language. The brothers were caught completely by surprise, and bowed down before him with their faces to the earth. (Gen. 42:6.)

Thus was the vision of Joseph's youth finally fulfilled. Who would have thought that a Hebrew youth who came to Egypt as a slave would ever be second in command to Pharaoh, ruling over all Egypt? To many it was impossible, but with God all things are possible.

When the brothers finally learned, on the second trip, that it was Joseph they were dealing with, they naturally became terrified, certain that he would have them all killed. Instead, he put all his Egyptian servants out of the room and broke down and wept with them. They tried to apologize, but Joseph insisted that it was the hand of God, and that what they had meant for evil, God was working for good. (Gen. 45:5.) God had worked such a transformation in Joseph's heart that all bitterness, self-pity and desire for revenge was gone. Joseph could forgive his brothers and welcome his family into Egypt.

If Joseph had disliked his father and brethren, or refused to forgive Potiphar and his wife, he never would have been the blesser. Those who hold onto bitterness are never blessers — they are only losers.

Joseph ended his life on target, fulfilling the vision of his youth, because he always kept his eyes on God and His promises, even when times were bad and it looked as if he were forsaken by God and man. He never let bitterness and rebellion enter his heart, but allowed God to work on him, transforming him into a vessel He could use for His glory in the earth.

I Pass the Sword to You

Joseph's test was typical of the tests you and I go through — the test of remaining faithful even when it seems that our God-given vision is not being fulfilled. Though God had confirmed the vision through a second dream, still Joseph's age nearly doubled while he was waiting for fulfillment — waiting and being faithful to God.

Visions — your vision included — are for an appointed time. They are God-given goals — destinations toward which our lives are to travel. How do you deal with the problems and delays in your life while you are waiting for the vision to be fulfilled? To answer that, answer this. How do you deal with the traffic lights, stop signs, intersections, traffic jams and detours when you are on a long trip? Do you not take them as they come, work your way through them, and continue toward your destination? Perhaps that is implied in God's instructions to Habakkuk: **. . . Write the vision, and make it plain upon tables, that he may run that readeth it** (Hab. 2:2).

The sword being passed to you may be in its sheath for a while. It may be that it will remain in its sheath while you are en route to an appointed destination at an appointed time. If so, keep the vision in plain view, read it often and keep running toward it.

21
Live a Life With Purpose

The Apostle Paul had a burning, driving purpose that kept him going on through persecutions, hardships and rejection. Nothing could stop him because he was determined to reach his goal and fulfill his purpose in life.

Nowhere else in his writing does he explain what motivated him as clearly as he does in his letter to the Philippians:

> But whatever former things I had that might have been gains to me, I have come to consider as (one combined) loss for Christ's sake.
>
> Yes, furthermore, I count everything as loss compared to the possession of the priceless privilege — the overwhelming preciousness, the surpassing worth and supreme advantage — of knowing Christ Jesus my Lord, and of progressively becoming more deeply and intimately acquainted with Him....
>
> Philippians 3:7,8 AMP

In the same passage, in verse 10, Paul says that his determined purpose is to know Christ. In verses 13 and 14 he says that he has not yet attained his purpose but he is pressing on.

Notice that he says that his purpose is to know Jesus and the power outflowing from His resurrection. (v. 10.) Often ministers get bogged down with some temporary goal and forget the larger purpose. Paul preached and saw many people born again, filled with the Holy Spirit and delivered from demon powers. He built many churches and had many great revelations which he taught and wrote down for future generations.

But Paul was careful never to glory in the things he had accomplished, or to see them as the purpose of his ministry and life. He told the Galatians, **But God forbid that I should glory, save in the cross of our Lord Jesus Christ...**(Gal. 6:14). Even when he defended his apostolic office to the Corinthians, he said that he would only glory in his infirmities that the power of God might be manifest. (2 Cor. 12:9.)

In 1 Thessalonians 2:13, the Apostle Paul instructs us: **For this cause also thank we God without ceasing, because, when ye received the word of God which ye heard of us, ye received it not as the word of men, but as it is in truth, the word of God, which effectually worketh also in you that believe.**

In 1 Samuel 17:29, David says to his brothers, **...Is there not a cause?** In Proverbs 26:2, the wise man Solomon writes, **...the curse causeless shall not come.** This means that there is a cause for every sickness, disease or blight.

In the world we live in, there must be a cause before there is an effect. Human nature always wants to work on effects, but never causes. We can have a blight such as AIDS that is becoming more of a plague every day, frightening humanity, but no one wants to deal with the cause of it. Everyone is interested in the effects, and will spend billions of dollars to eradicate the effects, yet ignore the cause. But every effect goes back to a cause.

Man's heart is where causes come into being, where causes are created. A great cause gives birth to great dreams, great activities, great fulfillment and great blessings. It begins with a cause down on the inside of a person.

The word "cause" comes from the Latin word *causa*, which means an occasion which creates a result. There must be an occasion and then a result of that occasion. First a cause and then an effect. The cause is a necessary antecedent for any effect. Without a cause there is no effect.

When we see all that is happening in the world today we are witnessing the effects, but behind it all there is a reason, a purpose and a cause. Cause determines change in things. From one cause you can have many effects.

Daniel Had a Purpose

Daniel was a young man, probably in his teenage years, when he was carried into captivity in Babylon with the first group of exiles. In Daniel 1:8 it says that he purposed in his heart not to defile himself with the king's fancy food and drink.

Daniel determined that though he had been carried off into captivity, he would not forget the laws of God. He would keep himself pure and trust God to take care of him. Daniel was willing to risk forfeiting his favored position in the court and possibly the wrath of the king by refusing to eat the king's fancy food. But he chose to honor and obey God, no matter what the consequences.

When life has a purpose, it will be tested as gold to see what is real and what is fake. Daniel was tested. God's favor was on him, and he was promoted high in the kingdom. Even as the king's close advisor, he maintained his prayer and devotional life. Other of the king's advisors were jealous of Daniel, and conspired to have an edict sealed by the king banning prayer to anyone except the king.

When Daniel heard of this ruling, he did not run and hide, but made it a point to pray as he always did, in plain sight, facing Jerusalem. His faith and purpose were severely tested as he was placed in a den of lions. But God intervened and closed the lions' mouths, vindicating Daniel's purpose and faith.

Shadrach, Meshach and Abed-nego

Daniel's three friends, Shadrach, Meshach and Abed-nego demonstrated their purpose when the king built his golden statue and commanded everyone in the province to bow down to it or face a burning, fiery furnace. These three men refused the king's demands, and told the king that they believed their God would deliver them, but even if He did not, they still would not bow down. (Dan. 3:17,18.)

Now that's commitment to a purpose, all the way! But God, true to His nature, met them in the fire and preserved them, without a hair of their heads being singed or even the smell of smoke on their clothes. The only thing they lost in the fire was the ropes that bound them.

God will meet you in the fire if you refuse to bow to pressures or temptations, and remain true to your purpose.

Moses Had a Purpose

Moses was one of the greatest men who ever lived. He was the lawgiver and deliverer of Israel, God's chosen instrument to bring them out of Egyptian bondage and to the Promised Land.

Moses lived his whole life by faith, with the purpose of God clearly before him. Hebrews 11 says that he was hid by faith as a baby, and that when he was come of years, he refused his earthly inheritance as Pharaoh's heir, choosing to suffer affliction with God's people, rather than enjoy the passing pleasure of sin. He esteemed the reproach of Christ greater riches than the treasures of Egypt, risking the wrath of the king because he looked on Him Who was invisible. (Heb. 11:23-27.)

How could Moses give up power, wealth and glory to lead a bunch of rebellious, stubborn people into the wilderness with the Egyptian army in hot pursuit? The only explanation is that Moses had a purpose. By faith, he knew he was called by God, and he believed that what God offered was better than all the kingdoms of this world put together.

People of Purpose Move the World

If Moses had remained in the royal court of Egypt, he would have been, at best, a footnote to history in some Egyptian pyramid. By sticking to his purpose and believing God, he became one of the central figures of history.

Men of purpose change the world. World revival cannot come about by compromise, but only by people who know their God and know their calling and refuse to compromise with the devil or the world.

Alexander the Great was asked how he conquered the world, and he replied, "I never wavered." Paul's determined purpose shook the Roman Empire. He told the Philippians:

> [For my determined purpose is] that I may know Him — that I may progressively become more deeply and intimately acquainted with Him, perceiving and recognizing and understanding [the wonders of His Person] more strongly and more clearly. And that I may in that same way come to know the power outflowing from His resurrection [which it exerts over believers]; and that I may so share His sufferings as to be continually transformed [in spirit into His likeness even] to His death....
> **Philippians 3:10** AMP

That same burning purpose to know Jesus Christ and the power outflowing from His resurrection carried over to men such as Martin Luther and John Wesley — men who shook the world in their generation. Oral Roberts is a living example of a man who has stood with his purpose and built a great university to train men and Christian leaders.

How Big Is Your Cause?

What are you doing today as a cause that will determine your end? Is your cause big enough? When you get further along in life, you will wonder what your cause is. Is it big enough for your destiny? You are going to have effects, and the effects are going to come from the cause.

Way down deep inside you are reaching for something — the ultimate drive and goal in your life. You have to determine if it is big enough for you. The effects are coming all around you, but are they the effects you want at the end of your life? If they are not, then you need to go back and see if your cause was big enough, or if it was insignificant.

Our pervasive cause in life is what makes us do what we do. There are great causes in life, and there are very weak causes in life. There is a cause before any effect. There has to be a cause before there can be an effect. We must determine what cause we are for in this life. God's heart is with the salvation of human souls. Our causes are where our great dreams are born, and we need to redirect our causes to where the heart of God is helping people. If we get our cause lined up with God's causes, we will change the world.

The Apostle Paul had a big cause to know Christ Jesus in the power of His resurrection and the fellowship of His sufferings. Paul knew that his cause was bigger than being born a Roman citizen, bigger than the great training in the Jewish law, bigger than the earthly glory and recognition that accompanied all the miracles God did through him and the churches he established. As Paul went to his death on the chopping block in Rome, he no doubt passed all the glory and splendor of the great Roman empire, but he could go rejoicing, at peace within, knowing, as he told Timothy, that he had fought the good fight, kept the faith and finished the course, and that there was laid up for him a crown of righteousness which the Lord would give him. (2 Tim. 4:7,8.) His cause cost him his life, but gained him everything.

The cause for which I stand is to bring men and women to the Savior, to their Lord and King — and to bring them to happiness and everlasting life. The effects of my cause are beautiful, happy, clean, good people. I urge you to have a great cause in living and a great cause in dying. Do not just live and die. Live and die on purpose. Live and die for a reason. Live and die doing something for Jesus' sake!

Find your purpose, and stay with it without compromise or retreat. God will use you to shake your generation if you will remain true to Him and the vision He gives you no matter what the cost or the obstacles.

What can you take from my words that will carry you forward in your obedience to God's call on your life? The Spirit of the Lord will, of course, quicken certain truths to your mind. Besides those, focus your thoughts on these three words: Purpose, purity and perseverance.

Your calling gives you purpose — and this purpose is the driving force of your life. In addition, your God-given purpose — and the hope of its fulfillment — will cause you to walk in purity. When you focus upon what God is making out of your life, you are filled with hope, and, **Everyone who has this hope in him purifies himself...**(1 John 3:3 NIV).

The crown, according to Revelation 2:10, goes to those who are faithful to their God-given purpose — the ones who persevere. Persevere in purity as you pursue your purpose!

Part IV
Take Up the Sword

22

The Secret of Greatness

I believe from the depths of my being that greatness is embedded in every one of us. Greatness has to do with certain principles. If we follow those principles, they become principles of greatness. There can be something more at the end of life than a tombstone.

Paul's Keys to Greatness

Paul had within him some native greatness. For example, he was born of religious parents. It is a tremendous asset in life to have good parents. Paul's parents put religious blood into his system. He called himself a Pharisee of the Pharisees.

Paul was born in Tarsus, a very commercial city. It was also an intellectual city with institutions of learning. Paul absorbed this community into himself. It would have been impossible for Peter to have become a Paul, because Peter was born in a provincial place in Galilee, and that provincialism never left him.

Paul was born in a world place with world thinking; ships from all over the world came into the port. As he met people from all cultures, Paul began to realize that God cared for everybody in the world. What a tremendous revelation.

Paul lived during the empire dominion of Rome, and was born with Roman citizenship, which was highly prized and paid for with great price by many in the empire at the time. (Acts 22:27,28.) He drank of empire feelings as he saw the returning armies with their trophies of world conquest at their feet.

But neither his Roman citizenship, nor his great training in the Jewish law under the feet of Gamaliel was what made Paul great. The secret of Paul's greatness was the decisions that he made.

Mediocre people make little decisions, or double decisions. On this side, they say one thing, then on the other side they say something else because they are trying to agree with everybody. If you are going to be great, you do not agree with anybody. If they want to agree with you, that is their business, but you say what you believe, and stick in there and believe it with all your heart. That is a form of greatness.

To determine the cause of Paul's greatness, we have to go back to what he said to the Romans and see the three things he said in Romans 1:14-16:

I am debtor both to the Greeks, and to the Barbarians; both to the wise, and to the unwise.

So, as much as in me is, I am ready to preach the gospel to you that are at Rome also.

For I am not ashamed of the gospel of Christ: for it is the power of God unto salvation to every one that believeth; to the Jew first, and also to the Greek.

Not Ashamed

Paul said that he was not ashamed of the Gospel of Christ, because it is the power of God unto salvation. Now we must be honest about this matter. If we were truly not ashamed of the Gospel, we would already have saved the world.

If the British government had not been ashamed of the Gospel, it would have remained a world empire. Many great nations of the past, such as France, Germany, Spain and Portugal had vast opportunities for world achievement and could have continued in their greatness if they had not become ashamed of the Gospel. If America were not ashamed of the Gospel, we could save the world. We are ashamed of prayer and Bible reading in our schools, and ashamed of exporting the Gospel to the world. We export pornography and other awful films, but we are ashamed of Jesus.

Paul boldly said, "I am not ashamed of the Gospel of Jesus Christ." He was talking to an empire that had thousands of gods, yet he held Jesus above them all and said, "I am not ashamed!" They had all kinds of mythology. They were following Zeus, Mars and so forth, yet Paul boldly proclaimed Jesus as Lord over all, even at the cost of great suffering, imprisonment and death.

I have been in more than one hundred nations of the world, and after seeing all the religions of the earth, I want to tell you that I am not ashamed of the Gospel of Jesus Christ. I looked at Communism for 5,000 miles across Russia and Siberia, and saw the slavery of the people. I would be ashamed of Communism, but I am not ashamed of the Gospel.

You can take all the great philosophies of mankind and exalt them with the wise words they say, but not one of them will save a soul from hell. Not one of them will lift a man higher than his bootstraps. But the Gospel of Jesus Christ will lift a man from the gutter of hopelessness and despair, give him something to live for and something to die for.

I Am Ready

Paul's second form of greatness was demonstrated when he said, "I am ready to preach to you there in your city." Paul was not only unashamed of the Gospel, but he was ready to preach it in Rome or the ends of the earth.

If there has been one sad mark on the Church for the last 2,000 years, it is that we have not been ready for anything. When Martin Luther came on the scene with a mighty message of justification by faith, the Church was not ready for it. In fact, they wanted to kill him. When John Wesley came on the scene with a mighty thrust of God in England, they were not ready for it. They cried, ''Throw him out! Destroy him!'' There were several cities in England that would put John Wesley in jail if he came within five miles of town. The world was not ready for him. Study every great man of God the world has known, and every time it is the same. The Church was not ready for them. Churches in this century have had opportunity after opportunity, and the answer is the same: ''We are not ready.''

Some of the most dramatic moments in world history have been the transferring of military power from a retiring general or king to a younger man. One of the saddest events in recent history occurred following World War II in Japan. General Douglas MacArthur ruled Japan, and the people looked to him as a god. Their gods had failed them, and they were spiritually bankrupt. MacArthur made an appeal to American churches to send him 10,000 Christian missionaries, and Japan would become a Christian nation. But the churches in America said, ''We are not ready.'' Less than a hundred missionaries responded to MacArthur's call, and today Japan is more un-Christian than ever.

Often God has spoken to individuals or groups to do something for Him, and the response has been, ''We are not ready.'' The truth is that if God did not think you were ready, He would not have asked you to do the thing in the first place. When we respond to God this way, we are saying, ''God, I am smarter than You. I know You asked me to do something, but I don't believe I am ready yet.''

By the time you get ready, the world will have changed so much that they will not need you anymore. When God says for you to do something, He does not mean for you to discuss it with some other person. He means for you to *do it!* He does not mean for you to run around looking for help. He just wants you to *do it!*

Paul the Debtor

The third thing that made Paul great is found at the beginning of our text, where Paul says, "I am a debtor." He had not borrowed any money, or bought a tent on credit. This was no physical indebtedness that he was talking about. He was talking about the greatest indebtedness in the world, which is spiritual and moral.

If a doctor found some great answer to disease and kept it to himself, he would not be great. If you develop some new invention or medical cure and try to sell it, you may be forgotten. But if you unselfishly give it to the world, you will never be forgotten.

Paul was a debtor to the world because of the abundance of revelation he received from God. He was compelled to share the revelation of Jesus Christ. He was a debtor to tell others how he was wonderfully converted and saved.

Until you can feel that moral indebtedness, and know that you are responsible for the man next door getting saved, until you feel that you cannot stop praying until the family across the street comes to Jesus, then you are not great.

The Church today has very little of that kind of feelings. What church today is burning for the salvation of America, believing they have to do something about it? What church feels that India has to be saved, and that they must do something to cause it to happen? If the entire Church in America would rise up as one, we could win the whole world in a short time. We have millions and millions of dollars stuffed away. The Church today must realize that we are debtors to the world, and we owe the world what we know and have. We owe the world our experiences, our knowledge and our goods.

Jesus told His disciples that as they had freely received, so they should freely give. We are responsible to give back from what we have received in such abundance. If we find a spring of living water, we are not supposed to just sit by it with a gun. We are supposed to share the living water with everyone who is thirsty. In a world without God, that is our responsibility.

The thing that made Paul truly great is that he took the responsibility for saving the world on himself. He ran from continent to continent, nation to nation and tribe to tribe, telling people that Jesus is Lord, and that all can come drink freely of the rivers of living water!

Paul's name is remembered long after the caesars were dead and buried, and their empire in ruins. You cannot rub Paul's name out. And the same will be true of any one of us who will refuse to be ashamed of the Gospel, be ready for whatever God is doing and saying and understand that we are debtors to the whole world, to share the message and ministry of reconciliation and salvation. Anyone who is willing to accept it can have true greatness.

23

What Is Your Personal Vision?

Every Christian has a vision from God — whether he accepts it or not. Parents have a vision to bring up their children in the faith and teach them right and wrong. Believers have a mandate and a vision to preach the Good News and to disciple the nations in the Kingdom of God. If every one of us would be faithful to our heavenly vision, we would take the world for Jesus!

Hang onto your vision. Be what God wants you to be.

I remember once lying on my bed and crying, ''God, send missionaries.'' And the Lord said, ''Yes, I'm sending you!'' He told me that if I would go, He would do more for me than ever before. I had to give up my church of a thousand members and go to a poor country devastated by war and poverty. And I had to act quickly.

If you don't act quickly, the devil will steal your vision. Keep the vision. Let the vision be bright.

God told me to preach, and that is what I do. He did not tell me to broadcast news. He told me to preach, and feed the hungry, and that is what I do.

If you have a vision, it is greater than money, or anything else the world can offer.

When I left my thousand-member church, the new pastor told me he might not have the church long, because God had called him to Bombay, India. I told him that was wonderful, but his wife didn't think so. She let out a scream and put her head against the wall. The people in the restaurant probably thought I had hit her. His wife said she was not going to Bombay. She was going to stay home with her car, refrigerator and comfortable bed. She refused to go. So her husband went to her, comforted her and told her it would be all right. What happened? They did not go to India. He later died of a heart attack, and she died of cancer. Was this God's best for them?

When God calls you, He means for you to obey. Every one of us has a vision. Are we going to end our lives like the Apostle Paul, saying that we have never been disobedient to the heavenly vision?

When God says to do something, you have to do it.

I was in Jerusalem recently, and God woke me up after midnight and shook me. I sat straight up in bed, and God said, "It's past midnight prophetically, too." That scared me. God said, "I want to tell you something. The people, My people, they sing about My coming. They preach about My coming and live as if I were never coming." I began to cry.

I said, "Oh, God, I'm so sorry. I'm so sad."

God said He was too. Then He began to talk to me. He said that Matthew 24 will now be fulfilled. Nation shall rise against nation, and kingdom against kingdom. There will be more and more earthquakes, and pestilence as we have never seen before. And there will be famines.

I listened to God, and then I asked Him why He didn't do something about it. He told me He wanted me to do something about it. He said He had children all over the world who were hungry and in need, and He loved them.

Like Moses, I began to quarrel with God. I reminded Him that I was an old man and had fulfilled my vision. I told Him to go talk to younger people coming on the scene.

He said no, that I was about old enough He could trust me now that I have lived in 110 nations and love the Third World people.

God's Visions Burn Like Fire

Remember this. When God puts in a new vision, it burns like fire, and most people don't understand it. Why would I want to be away from my family and my beautiful church? I speak to six or seven million people every morning, on satellite, covering North America. I thought I was busy, but God said, "a new vision."

You may be doing what God told you to do today, and in one night, God will come and change your vision to a brand new one, and He will want you to respond.

The Vision of God Burns Inside

The vision of God is different from your education, or from what you can learn naturally. It burns on your insides and will not stop until it is fulfilled. If you do not fulfill it, you don't sleep well and you get afraid to die. So it is better to be obedient to the heavenly vision.

It doesn't matter what you are doing or how well off or successful you are. When God plants a vision, He wants you to respond. Whether you are a preacher or a member of the choir — or a lazy pew-sitter — God has a vision for your life. Just for you. No one will have one like yours. But the vision is from God. Walk in the vision. Live the vision, and in heaven you will rejoice. You will be glad, because you obeyed God.

The vision must live forever in our hearts.

One of my burning visions is that I must hand over the sword to a new generation. I must impart to them the simple, incredible truth: *God wants you!*

Why has God given me such a burden? Well, as I search the Bible, I see so many examples of how the Lord put a similar burden on other men He had chosen. I look to the Apostle Paul. I admire the time and trouble he took with the young preacher Timothy. What an honor he paid this faithful young minister — by writing to him two books of the Bible, 1 and 2 Timothy. Read those books if you have never before. They are a gentle, encouraging, and personalized instruction from a grand old man to a fiery young newcomer.

In 2 Timothy 2:15, Paul commended Timothy in his first period of apprenticeship: **Study to shew thyself approved unto God, a workman that needeth not to be ashamed, rightly dividing the word of truth.** That is such a powerful verse.

Another wise truth is found in 2 Timothy 1:6. Paul encouraged young Timothy to **. . .stir up the gift of God, which is in thee by the putting on of my hands.** What does that mean? Well, let's go to the Greek and look at the preceding verse, too — and the verse after it.

What is Paul saying to his young disciple? In plain English, he is saying:

''Timothy, I am filled with memories of the sincere faith that you have shown ever since I met you. It is the same, deep faith I saw in your grandmother, Lois, and your mother, Eunice. It dwells in your heart, too. That's why I now remind you to keep ever blazing that flame of special grace, that divine gift God has graciously given to you, which came upon you when I laid my hands on you.

''God has not given us a spirit of fear and timidity. We are not to shrink from danger. We are not cowards. No, the spirit He gave us is of strength, love and self-discipline — self-restraint and wise discretion.''

The Amplified New Testament puts verse 7 like this: **. . .[He has given us a spirit] of power and of love and of calm and well-balanced mind and discipline and self-control.** What powerful advice to a young preacher!

I also love what Paul wrote to his young ward in 1 Timothy 1:19: **Holding faith, and a good conscience; which some having put away concerning faith have made**

shipwreck. He warned the young man that some had put away their faith and become spiritually shipwrecked.

Going back to the original Greek, basically, Paul said in 1 Timothy 1:18,19:

''This is the charge or order or command that I entrust to you, Timothy, my son, in agreement with the prophecies that first directed me to you. Fight the good fight. Cling tightly to your faith and keep your conscience clear. By ignoring their consciences certain persons have run aground. They have wrecked their witness and crashed their ministries into the rocks.''

Are you listening to this?

I wish that some of my preacher friends had taken this passage a bit more seriously. Perhaps we could have avoided some of the scandals of the last few years!

This is for you, too! Listen to what Paul is saying! *You should listen to your conscience.*

Faith Unfeigned

In 1 Timothy 1:5, Paul said that young Timothy must have faith unfeigned. What does ''faith unfeigned'' mean? Paul was demanding simple sincerity and not hypocritical presumptuous living.

In verse 6 he continues, as elsewhere, to show the consequence: ...**some having swerved have turned aside unto vain jangling.** Paul instructed that if you leave honest and simple faith, you will turn yourself from the road of salvation, swerve another direction, and turn aside into big trouble.

Are you listening?

In 1 Timothy 4:6, the great apostle admonished Timothy to be nourished in the words of faith. *Faith comes by hearing, and hearing comes by the Word of God,* proclaims Romans 10:17. Faith is maintained through prayer, witnessing and fellowship with godly people. Paul said to keep yourself nourished and strong in the words of faith.

In 1 Timothy 4:1, Paul showed Timothy how the Holy Ghost speaks expressly that in the latter times, ...**some shall** *depart from the faith,* **giving heed to seducing spirits, and doctrines of devils.** This verse needs no interpretation. The Holy Ghost said that in the last days there would be those who would walk away from the teachings of the Church and the simple doctrines of Jesus Christ. His admonition was, "Don't depart from your original faith!"

These two little books are full of such wisdom!

In 1 Timothy 4:12, the great apostle commanded Timothy to be an example in his faith. This is for us today. We are not to do as others do, but we are to teach them what to do.

Examine carefully the powerful warning in 1 Timothy 6:10: **For the love of money is the root of all evil: which while some coveted after, they have erred from the faith, and pierced themselves through with many sorrows.**

I have seen so many friendships destroyed by unfaithfulness over money. Terrible things happen when we decide that money is more important than people! When we love money, nothing good can result. Loving money leads to all kinds of evil. In their eagerness to be rich, so many men of God have fallen into total disgrace.

Money is not the problem. Loving money more than loving people is. What an explosion of truth to a young disciple! Coveting money will cause you to wander into all kinds of temptation, err from the faith and be pierced through with many sorrows.

Paul followed this up by crying unto Timothy, "Man of God, flee these things." (v. 11.)

Then in 2 Timothy 3, Paul gives one of the most powerful bits of advice that any young Christian can ever receive. Listen, my friend: Here is a warning that is timeless. It is prophetic, too. It describes our day so clearly. In verses 1-4 Paul tells Timothy to realize that there are going to be hard times in the final days in which it is going to be very difficult to be a Christian. In those days, Paul warns, people will be selfish and utterly self-centered. They will be lovers of money, boastful, arrogant gossips, full of big words, with no respect for their parents, no gratitude, no reverence to God.

Does this sound at all familiar? Have you turned on prime-time television lately? This describes the culture that Hollywood apparently envisions for America!

Paul warns of a time when people will be without natural affection, unforgiving, delighted with scandal, lacking self-control, hating good, loving violence. He says they will be treacherous, headstrong, conceited, blinded with pride and loving pleasure more than God. He is describing our day!

Then, in verse 5, he begins to describe our modern Church! He says they will maintain a facade of religion, but it will be a false piety. Yes, they will go to church, but they will turn their backs on the power of God. Paul warned his dear Timothy, **. . . from such turn away.** That goes for you, too.

Beware! Such times are here and now. The warning is for you.

Faith Is a Fight

In 1 Timothy 6:12, the apostle said, **Fight the good fight of faith, lay hold on eternal life. . . .** Then in verses 13 and 14 he said:

> **I give thee charge in the sight of God, who quickeneth all things. . . .**

That thou keep this commandment without spot, unrebukeable, until the appearing of our Lord Jesus Christ.

Yes! You, too, are to keep up the good fight for the faith! You are to hold tightly to your salvation. Paul told Timothy that he commanded him before Almighty God, the Source of all things Who protects us all, that Timothy was to steer clear of evil, to keep himself untouched by scandal, to avoid all shame.

I remember being in Israel, in the city of Jericho, looking down into the Jordan valley toward the mountains of Moab. If you look as far as the eye can see, the highest point there is Mt. Nebo. That's where God led Moses after he had led the children of Israel out of Egyptian bondage, then through the wilderness for forty years. God got Moses up on Mt. Nebo and said, "I want you to look down across the Jordan, and I want you to see that fertile plain of the Jordan valley and all of its lush greenery with deserts on either side." And He said, "Moses, you're not going to be able to go over there." Why? Because Moses had disobeyed. He had not steered clear of evil. He had given into pride.

We do not *make* God perform miracles. I believe in faith. I thank God for the faith message! But I believe it is time in the Body of Christ when we take what we have learned of this tremendous message of faith and begin to add to it the action of aggressive faith-filled prayer. It is time to take the message of faith across the Jordan, out of the mountains of Moab, out of Mt. Nebo.

For forty years, Moses' shoes did not wear out. Now, when it happens to us, we are so proud! Let's come down and cross the Jordan and go into enemy-held territory and stop showing each other our shoes that don't wear out, because it's no good to have shoes that don't wear out if you are not going anywhere.

It is time for us to change from a ministry of maintaining to a ministry of obtaining. Yes! It is time to charge into enemy-held territory and reclaim what rightfully belongs to us. We have come into spiritual Jerusalem, and it is time to take possession of our Promised Land.

Jesus did not die on the cross so that you or I can have lives of luxury and a million dollars in the bank! The message of faith is abused and misused when we only concentrate on giving *ourselves* prosperity and great personal wealth. Faith should be used to win others to salvation. It's time for ministries to use their multi-million-dollar offerings to evangelize the world!

In 1 Timothy 5:12, Paul speaks of those who have cast off their first faith. It is a great pity to have faith, to use faith and then to cast it off in favor of greed.

24

The Joy of Passing the Sword

One of the most exciting stories about passing the sword is found in 2 Kings, Chapter 2.

For ten years Elisha had lived in the presence of the prophet Elijah. He had worked hard as Elijah's servant and had watched this mighty prophet of God work miracles. He followed his master with great fidelity. No doubt, he slept at his feet at night, and if his master needed anything, he would get it for him. He was there when Jezebel and the prophets of Baal screamed against Elijah, and he was there when Elijah raised the dead.

At the dramatic moment of the passing of the sword, they came to the Jordan River, and with the wave of Elijah's cloak, the water of the Jordan parted to let them cross on dry land. In the desert Elijah asked his servant Elisha, "What do you want?"

Here was a great opportunity. Elisha could have asked for a high position in government, a magnificent home filled with servants or pockets filled with gold, but he did not. Instead, Elisha said, "I want a double portion of your spirit."

Elijah replied, "If you see me when I go away, you will have it."

Suddenly Elisha saw heaven's horses and chariots of fire descending from the sky. The Holy Spirit separated Elijah from Elisha. Elijah climbed aboard the chariot of fire and dropped his old cloak as he sped away with new garments from heaven. No one except Elisha has ever beheld such a scene. As Elijah waved good-bye, he no doubt grasped his hand and admonished Elisha, "Hold the sword, young man."

Elisha tore off his own garments of personal achievement and goodness and threw them in the desert. He picked up the garment of divine authority and wrapped it around his shoulders. It fit perfectly. Arriving at the Jordan river with great courage, Elisha did the same thing. He hit the water with the cloak of Elijah and commanded it to part, and the water obeyed him.

This is one of the greatest transitions of power in history. It has to do with the older communicating his authority, anointing and blessing to the younger. How beautiful it is to pass the sword of strength unto another generation. The Christian energy I feel as I pass the sword to you was expressed by the Apostle Paul in these words:

> ...I am...eager to preach the gospel....
>
> **because it is the power of God for the salvation of everyone who believes....**
>
> Romans 1:15,16 NIV

This same Christian energy can enable you to carry the sword triumphantly into victorious battle if you, child of God, will do as Paul exhorts: ...**flee from all this** [temptation], **and pursue righteousness, godliness, faith, love, endurance and gentleness. Fight the good fight of the faith. Take hold of the eternal life to which you were called**...(1 Tim. 6:11,12 NIV).

As you accept the sword, you must know that you are in the driver's seat, steering your life and fulfilling your call under the anointing and leadership of the Holy Spirit. No enemy who rises before you can overcome you, for you ...**are from God and have overcome them**...**because the one who is in you is greater than the one who is in the world** (1 John 4:4 NIV).

Hallelujah!

Now, let me share with you a favorite theory of mine that, no, I cannot find anywhere in the Bible. This is just Brother Lester Sumrall speaking now. I have found that our life spans are divided into three very important periods.

1 Your Receiving or Getting Period

The first period of your life I call your *receiving period*. This time span is approximately from birth to thirty years of age. During this time your parents, other family members, your playmates and your teachers in school all constantly plant information or education into your mind. You are in the greatest learning period of your life. You receive a wealth of diverse sorts of information. This time period actually determines the second and third portions of your human story.

This first phase is most important to your final destiny. It could be the most exciting period of your life because learning is exciting. You are not only being trained physically, but morally, spiritually and mentally. It is your receiving period that makes you what you are. It is so important that you receive the right material into your mind, because the determinations you make during this period will decide your eternity.

2 Your Using Period

The second period of your life is from approximately age thirty to age sixty. This second period is the *using period*. During these very fruitful years you dispense the knowledge, experience and wealth of information gained in the first thirty years of life. These could be called your most productive years, for almost every moment you choose to use what you have already learned.

Of course, this is a very important portion of your life. You have received instruction from your parents, grandparents and school teachers, and now you are hammering this knowledge into a frame. This is certainly an exciting opportunity to use all the abilities that you have accumulated from zero to thirty years.

3 Your Giving Out Period

The third period with a full life extends from age sixty to age seventy and beyond. This is the *giving out* period of your life. You obtained it and learned it and it was successful, and now you want to replant it into a new generation. This could be the happiest time schedule of your life, because now you are giving away what you have learned and used.

This is the way I came to know Smith Wigglesworth. He was past eighty and I was about twenty-five. That meant that he was in his final giveaway period of life. He knew he had received some things from the Lord, and he desired to share them with a younger man. In fact, he was delighted to give it away, and I was glad to receive it.

To visit with Smith Wigglesworth was to sense the greatness of his spirit. He was not like someone acting before an audience, or talking to a crowd of people. He was very relaxed and wanted to talk about the very intimate situations in his ministry. As he told of his various exploits of faith, including delivering many people from epileptic seizures, something would rise up in the hearer and cause him to want to do that also.

These two types of people get along so well; one in the first period of receiving and the other in the third period of giving. This makes devoted friends; one has it and the other wants it. I came to love Smith Wigglesworth very much during the two years I lived in England.

With Howard Carter it was a different story. We met when I was twenty years old and he was in his giant *using* period. I saw him lay hands on an entire Bible school of students, and every one of them received the infilling of the Holy Spirit immediately. I saw him lay hands upon groups of ministers to impart the gift of prophecy and the gift of interpretation of tongues, and each one received. I watched him train nations all around the world. I was in my learning period, learning from him and others as we traveled around the world. He was in his using period and was ministering on the gifts of the Spirit.

As I look upon my life, I see how important it is for a young minister to receive blessings, wisdom and knowledge from those who have gone through that period of life. So, don't miss the greatest blessings of life by being a loner. If someone paves a road, ride on it! After all, we are one Body in Christ.

Farewell to Arms

Passing the sword to younger officers is a traditional operation in the world's military system. Perhaps some of the most exciting scenes of history have been when the sword of authority is passed from one high-ranking officer, upon his retirement from the military, to younger men whom he has trained to be captains, colonels and generals.

In Israel, all officers of the Israeli military are handed the sword on the peak of Masada where the zealots held out against the Roman army for several months.

Alexander the Great, a young man who had conquered the mighty armies of the earth, lay dying. In his farewell to arms, he divided his world power among four of his greatest generals. His Greek empire ruled the earth for many years. What an awesome scene this must have been with all the regalia of court observing the transition of power.

I think of the great general and emperor, Napoleon Bonaparte, and I wonder about the intensity of the moment when he called his fighting generals around him, men who had been with him through many devastating wars, seeing many of their comrades killed in action, and told them, "Gentlemen, generals, farewell to arms. We shall never meet again as an organized group of military men. This is the day of my release from active duty. I wish to thank you for your courage. I wish to thank you for your determination. Above all else, I wish to thank you for your loyalty to me and to our country. Gentlemen, farewell to arms!"

One of the most sensational farewell to arms in this century is that of the forced retirement of Gen. Douglas MacArthur from the American military. Those generals, colonels, captains and sergeants had fought with him from Australia, island by island. They had freed many nations, including Indonesia, Malaysia, Singapore, the Philippines, Hong Kong, Taipei and on to Tokyo. Behind them was a string of blood — American blood, Japanese blood and the blood of nationals. MacArthur stood erect as usual and spoke clearly to these officers of the military:

"Farewell to arms. You have been a noble lot. You have followed me closely. You obeyed my commands and we won island after island with great suffering. You did more than was expected of you. Your names will go down in history as strong, courageous men.

"Gentlemen, I have been recalled by the president of the United States from active duty, and at this moment, I must say, 'farewell to arms' to you. We shall never on this earth gather again as the same military group. In a few moments, we will no longer be linked together by position, but only by being Americans. Farewell."

There were not many dry eyes as a great fighting general passed his sword to those who were younger, to those who had fought alongside him. What a traumatic termination of service as one delivers the sword of justice, of honor and of strength to subordinates who say, "Don't stop here, but go on to the higher plateaus of victory and glory.''

Passing the Sword of Integrity

One of the most remarkable persons in the Old Testament is the prophet Samuel. His destiny was very unusual as he was born by a miracle. His mother was barren. She was so overwhelmed by her barren situation that she was in church weeping desperately. Eli the priest prayed over her and she promised that the son to be born to her would serve in the priesthood. Nine months later she gave birth to a man child and called him Samuel.

Samuel lived in the holy tabernacle of God and was the equivalent of a modern-day altar boy. He possibly was also a servant to the priest, to bring him water or wash his hands, or otherwise minister to him. He grew up knowing more about God than anyone else, carefully observing all the functions and operations of the holy ceremonies of the tabernacle of Jehovah. When he was very young, possibly less than ten years old, God spoke to him and he replied, ''Here am I.'' This was the beginning of a lifelong communication between this remarkable child and God.

At the death of the old regime when Eli fell backward with the bad news that the battle had been lost, broke his neck and died, Samuel became the political leader of the nation. He governed in political and spiritual matters, as the last judge and as a prophet of God. He lived a wonderful life, in close relationship with God, fully clothed in the armor of God. But, Samuel lived in a time of changing attitudes among the people. The Israelites looked at the surrounding nations and decided they needed a king, and not just a judge and prophet. They demanded a royal family like the nations around them had.

In his final address to the nation and the handing over and passing of the sword, Samuel spoke to that nation in the strongest possible words. With the rulers and the great men of the nation standing before him, he said, "I wish to challenge this nation before I die to a final examination of my life. I have taken nothing from you. I have stolen nothing from you. I have not taxed you."

As he handed over the sword to another generation and anointed a man named Saul to be king over Israel, Samuel challenged him to walk before God and to live for God. The anointing was so strong that the young man Saul began to prophesy — a remarkable thing for a king to be doing.

It is amazing how this tremendous person handed over the leadership of a nation, and passed the sword unto the kings of Israel that lasted for many centuries.

You cannot give what you do not have. If you once had the power and anointing of God, but have retired and quit using it, you have nothing to pass on to others. You can only pass on what you are using at the time of the passing of the sword.

Possibly Moses' was one of the greatest transitions of power. He lived forty years in the palaces of Egypt as the son of Pharaoh's daughter. He was fully accepted as an Egyptian of the royal family. He fled from Egypt into the desert of Sinai. For the second forty years, God spoke to him. He became a shepherd in the desert. At eighty years of age he was called by God to bring deliverance to possibly three million Israelites in slavery in Egypt. By the wisdom and power of God, Moses brought those people forth out of Egypt toward the Promised Land.

For forty years Moses led these people — until he was 120 years of age. Then God said that it was time for him to leave the earth. Moses gave one of the most amazing dissertations man has ever heard, telling his nation how to live and act. The day of his departure for heaven, he laid his hands upon Joshua, his successor, and prayed for him as he passed the sword to him. It was one of the most dramatic days in the history of mankind. He instructed Joshua on how to live and fight, and told him that the spirit of Moses would rest on him.

When passing the sword to the younger man, Moses turned and climbed the mountain with his own strength. With God's binoculars he looked over the whole area where the twelve tribes would reside, then lay down and went to heaven. Almighty God took the time to bury his bones.

Passing the sword is so real, and so necessary.

Jesus Passes the Sword

Another remarkable transition took place in Jerusalem. In Mark 16:14, the Lord Jesus upbraided the disciples for their unbelief and hardness of heart. This really grabbed their attention because they thought they had great faith and great tenderness. Jesus was preparing them for verses 15 and 16:

> ...**Go ye into all the world, and preach the gospel to every creature.**

> **He that believeth and is baptized shall be saved; but he that believeth not shall be damned.**

Then in Acts 1:8, His last words to them were, **But ye shall receive power, after that the Holy Ghost is come upon you: and ye shall be witnesses unto me both in Jerusalem, and in all Judea, and in Samaria, and unto the uttermost part of the earth.**

This was His transition of power to His disciples. These were unbelievable promises from the Lord Jesus Christ and the handing over of leadership, or passing the sword, to the Church. This leadership role became evident in Acts 2 when they received the Holy Spirit, and Peter spoke to the people, with the result of over three thousand souls being born again.

In the next chapter the first great miracle of the early Church occurred with the healing of the lame man. The disciples knew that Jesus had really passed the sword on to them now. What He did, they could do. All the instruction they had received from Jesus over three and one-half years would now be usable in establishing the Kingdom of God.

Possibly no religious leader in all of history ever performed on such a grand scale as Jesus in that He did not pass the sword to one person but to many. In the upper room, 120 accepted or received the sword, to go into all the world and convert all people to the leadership of the Lord Jesus Christ.

I Pass the Sword to You

When God was leading Israel through anointed and chosen men, there came times for changes in leadership — the passing of the sword from one anointed person to another. It was also true in the New Testament Church, and it is true in the Church today. The very fact that you are reading this book probably indicates that the Spirit of the Lord is drawing you to take part in the changing of the guard — the passing of the sword.

I challenge you to determine where you are in this vital transition. Is the sword in your hand? Is your hand experienced, trained and proven with a track record of victories? Is yours a hand that has been in the thick of the battle? Has your hand brandished the sword, blazing new trails of victorious conquest for the Kingdom of God? Are you convinced by the Spirit of the Lord that the time has come for you to give out to younger warriors in the Kingdom?

Only a clear yes to these questions can place you in the time of life for you to replant what you have learned into a new generation.

Is your hand firmly clinched to the sword? Are your spiritual eyes alert to the enemy and fixed on a vision — that guiding star — given you by the Lord? Do your waking moments find you consumed in spiritual conflict and conquest? Are your nights of rest punctuated by burdened intercession?

If these questions bring a yes to your spirit, then you are probably in your period of greatest usefulness in the advancing army of God. Don't withdraw from the battle when the anointing is on you to fight and win.

Is your hand reaching for the sword? Does every report of victory in the Kingdom stir your inward being to march into the battle? Do the war stories of veterans experienced in the work of the Lord write themselves on the pages of the spiritual journal tucked away in the secret place of your heart? Do you find yourself mentally role playing and identifying with the man of God who shares reports of setting captives free?

Then you are being prepared and equipped as you reach for the sword.

Knowing the right time is vital. Moses' experience illustrates this well. Early in his life, he had it in his heart that he was to lead the children of Israel out of Egypt. When he took it upon himself to do it prematurely, he was forced to flee as a fugitive from justice. Later, when he was instructed by the Lord that the time had come to fulfill his calling, he returned to Egypt and left as a victor. He entered Egypt in the minority, but he departed in the majority.

When do you grasp the sword? As it was with the eleven who heard Jesus say, ...**Go ye into all the world, and preach the gospel to every creature**...(Mark 16:15), you too must hear your Commander's instruction that your apprenticeship is completed and it is time for you to grasp the sword and march toward the enemy with the sword of the Spirit, which is the Word of God. (Eph. 6:17.)

25
Our God Is Mighty!

I found Howard Carter.

If you remember from Chapter 18, I left him in Arkansas, then returned home to deliver my sister to our parents. Then, as quickly as I could, I hurried to California to join him on his missionary trip around the world.

But where was he?

If you recall, the Lord showed me that he was not in Japan or China or India where different people told me he had gone. No, the Lord told me to go to Australia. And I obeyed — spending almost every cent I had to my name.

Well, it was a long and difficult voyage with several stopovers. As our ship steamed into New Zealand for a thirty-six hour stopover on the way to Australia, I was praying, "Where is he?"

Little did I know that Howard Carter was praying, too. What was his prayer? The same as mine: "Where is he, Lord? Where is that young man that You said was going to be my helper? I have lost track of him. Where is that young man who was supposed to meet me in California?"

The Lord spoke to him that I was on a boat pulling into Wellington harbor that very minute. Wellington is the capital of New Zealand, and Carter was then also en route to Australia. He was preaching up in a rural mountain area of New Zealand and intended to stay there for several more weeks. So, guided by the Spirit telling him that I was arriving that very day in New Zealand, Carter wrote me a note saying, "Go on to Australia and minister until I arrive. We will travel from Sydney together." Then, he asked one of the preachers with him to go back home to Wellington and give me the note.

Do you sense the enormous faith of Howard Carter? He just knew that I was, indeed, in Wellington and that this preacher would find me with no trouble.

Wellington is a big city. The next morning, I left the ship to look around. After all, I had never been to New Zealand. I asked a complete stranger on the street, "Is there a church in this city where people say 'Hallelujah' and 'Praise the Lord' in church?"

He pointed across a railroad track and up a little hill in the distance. I followed his directions and found a small church. My knock on the door of the parsonage was answered by none other than the preacher Carter had just sent back to town the night before.

"Excuse me," I said. "You don't know who I am, but..."

"Yes, I do," he said. "You're Lester Sumrall."

I nearly fainted.

"How could you know?"

He gave me Carter's note.

Chills Ran Up and Down My Spine

This Howard Carter was so spiritual that it was spooky. If I had given it much thought, I probably would have decided I didn't want to be around anybody like that. How could I ever live up to him?

I thanked the pastor and returned to my ship. Obediently, I continued on to Australia. I had spent most of my remaining twelve dollars. The prophecy of the preacher back in California had been ringing in my ears. Yes, I was about to be stranded — where I would almost certainly starve to death.

But that was not what God had in mind. He watched to see if I would obey. I did. I trusted in Him for everything. I obeyed Carter's instructions to go and minister while I waited for him. I preached in Melbourne, then in the town of Bendigo. The Lord provided money and I rented a tent and preached in Brisbane for six weeks with all sorts of dramatic results. Then, I returned to Sydney and spent Christmas with a church there, holding a week of meetings with great outpourings of God's blessing which climaxed with a watch night service on New Year's Eve.

After very little sleep on New Year's Day, 1935, I heard that there was an American ship pulling into the harbor. I went down to the wharf, but did not see Howard Carter. With a heavy heart, I turned away. For some reason, however, I stopped at the customs shed — I guess just to check for certain. I looked up and there was Howard Carter grinning at me.

"Well, I am glad to see you," he said.

I was certainly glad to see him. My life was never the same again. From Australia to Indonesia to Singapore to Hong Kong, he and I began our two and one-half year journey together. In primitive Java, I encountered demon possession for the first time — and was forced to confront the devil. Fortunately, Carter was on hand to advise me that although I did not want to be a "devil-chasing" preacher, I should accept the portion God was giving to me.

What wisdom. Instead of fighting, I obeyed.

While riding in a mule-train caravan, we ministered in the Communist-infested hinterlands of China where we were captured by bandits then miraculously released. We ministered in Japan then crossed back into icy Manchuria for a trans-Siberia train ride through Russia into Poland. From there, we preached in pre-World War II Europe. We preached in Nazi Germany, Holland, the Scandinavian countries and the British Isles, ministering salvation, healing, deliverance and Holy Spirit baptism.

My time with Howard Carter was invaluable. He was a great teacher of the Word of God, especially in the area of the operation and gifts of the Holy Spirit. He had much prior experience and maturity, and a great compassion for the lost of the world. I learned from him to build a firm foundation on the written Word of God and to pursue the vision God had given me without getting sidetracked on issues and personal ambition.

Howard Carter taught me to think constantly on the Word of God and to be consistent in my work. In all my life I have never met a person who worked in the ministry as hard as Howard Carter. He was either studying and writing or preaching. He would cause very simple truths to become lofty. I could say that in many ways I "grew up" under Howard Carter.

Why Did the Lord Send Me to Him?

I believe there were many reasons, but among them, the Lord saw my impatience, my youthful exuberance — and the danger I was in of being a flash in the pan. I could have been a shooting star — which brightens the night sky only for a moment, then is gone. Instead the Lord wanted me (and you!) to be like the true stars of the sky:

> **And the teachers and those who are wise shall shine like the brightness of the firmament; and those who turn many to righteousness — to uprightness and right standing with God [shall give forth light] like the stars for ever and ever.**
>
> **Daniel 12:3 AMP**

The Holy Spirit says that those who bring many to righteousness today will shine like the stars forever. When Jesus talked about His return He said that the righteous will shine forth as the sun. (Matt. 13:43.)

In my years of ministry around the world, I have seen different kinds of stars. Some men and leaders are like the great, guiding North Star, and others are like brief shooting stars.

The North Star has remained in place since man has been on the earth. Its brilliance is permanent. Its light has been available for every generation. Millions have been saved by that star. Mariners set their compass by it. The North Star is dependable.

Shooting stars shine brighter when they appear, but they do not last but a second. They are bright, noisy and spectacular, shooting across the sky in a dramatic way. But they fade away and are of no value.

The Bible gives many examples of shooting stars and North Stars. Paul told the Corinthians that the things written in the Old Testament were written for examples to us, on whom the ends of the world have come. (1 Cor. 10:11.)

One such example is the story of Samuel and Saul. Both men were called and anointed by God, one as a prophet-judge and the other as the first king over Israel. Samuel stayed true to God and was a North Star, giving light and direction to God's people, even after his death, while Saul became a shooting star, shining bright for a few years then fizzling into rebellion, sin and destruction.

Samuel was a North Star because he was a great intercessor before God. He stood on behalf of the people and even tried to talk God out of letting them have a king, because he knew the problems and grief it would cause. (1 Sam. 8.) The Holy Spirit, speaking to Jeremiah, put Samuel on a plane with Moses because of his intercession for the people of Israel. (Jer. 15:1.)

Saul, on the other hand, started out with great promise, but soon became a shooting star that faded away. Saul began very humbly, hiding among the baggage when it was time to proclaim him king. (1 Sam. 10:21,22.) However, he soon let pride enter in, and his rebellion against God caused the Lord to reject him as king and to look to another tribe and family for His anointed.

The crisis came when God told Saul to completely destroy the Amalekites, including all people and cattle. Saul saved the best of the cattle and spared the life of King Agag. This so grieved God that He regretted making Saul king. (1 Sam. 15:11.) When Samuel heard from God what Saul had done, and that God had rejected Saul, it so grieved him that he cried to the Lord all night. (1 Sam. 15:11.) This was another mark of Samuel's greatness. He never had an ''I told you so'' spirit that tried to justify itself. Instead, he was grieved with God over Saul's rebellion.

Samuel then confronted Saul with his sin. Saul immediately tried to deny it. When Samuel asked about the cattle he heard in the background, Saul said that the people kept some to sacrifice, to which Samuel replied:

> **...Hath the Lord as great delight in burnt offerings and sacrifices, as in obeying the voice of the Lord? Behold, to obey is better than sacrifice, and to hearken than the fat of rams.**
>
> **For rebellion is as the sin of witchcraft, and stubbornness is as iniquity and idolatry....**
> **1 Samuel 15:22,23**

This is an established principle written down for our admonition and instruction. Saul was offering a sacrifice to God, just as the law of Moses commanded. But God had specifically told him to destroy all those cattle. Saul was in rebellion and leading the people in rebellion, and God called that witchcraft and idolatry.

Young man, young woman, follow the example of Samuel. Stay true to God so He can make you a North Star, shining like a beacon of hope and stability.

What Makes a Shooting Star?

Men become shooting stars when they get their focus off the Word of God and winning the lost, and start camping on some pet doctrine or special revelation. Whole churches, associations and denominations become shooting stars. They start bright with a true move of the Holy Spirit, then start dividing over legalistic traditions and soon fade away and loose their effectiveness.

Focus on the Lost

In these last days, as we see Bible prophecy fulfilled in the daily newspaper headlines, there is a temptation to focus on what is happening and to start looking for the Rapture as an escape. That is dangerous, and will cause us to fizzle out like a shooting star. Jesus spoke about the end of the age:

> **And this gospel of the kingdom shall be preached in all the world for a witness unto all nations; and then shall the end come.**
>
> **Matthew 24:14**

Addressing the same subject, James says:

> **Be patient therefore, brethren, unto the coming of the Lord. Behold, the husbandman waiteth for the precious fruit of the earth, and hath long patience for it, until he receive the early and latter rain.**
>
> **James 5:7**

Jesus told His disciples that the harvest is plenteous but the laborers are few, and He admonished them and us to pray to the Lord of the harvest that He would send forth workers. (Matt. 9:37,38.) God created man to fellowship with Him, and He loved His creation so much that He gave His only Son to redeem man from eternal death and separation from the Creator. God's primary purpose throughout history has been the redemption of man. When we lose sight of this fact and start emphasizing some new doctrine or revelation, even if it is biblical and good, we get off God's track and become shooting stars that will fizzle out and fade away.

Jesus asked His disciples if, when the Son of Man returned, He would find faith on the earth. (Luke 18:8.) When Jesus returns He expects to find us trusting Him and busy bringing in the harvest of souls to the Kingdom. Keep your foundation firm on the Word of God and the focus of your ministry on winning the lost of the world to Jesus, and you will not be a shooting star that fades away, but a North Star that is fixed in place — a steady and dependable beacon of truth and light in a dark world.

Decide To Be a North Star

Each of us must decide either to be a shooting star, seeking to gain notoriety and publicity in a ministry for a short time, or, lighted by the energy of heaven, humble to walk in the ways of God, to be like a North Star guiding travelers of destiny toward the New Jerusalem:

But the path of the just is as the shining light, that shineth more and more unto the perfect day.
Proverbs 4:18

The sword that I pass to you — the ministry of the Gospel of the Lord Jesus Christ — is not about us, it is about the lost. It is not about the Church, it is about the world. It is not about meetings, seminars and growth conferences, it is about getting the message to the lost. It is not about televangelism, it is about ...**the gospel** [that] **must...be preached to all nations** (Mark 13:10 NIV).

To get caught up in the methods and the media is to turn our attention to what we are doing, and to ourselves. It is to become, not a guiding star, but a shooting star. As faithful stewards of the sword, we must forever be caught up in the Great Commission, joining the Apostle Paul in

176

saying to the world: . . . **We implore you on Christ's behalf: Be reconciled to God** (2 Cor. 5:20 NIV).

26

I Am Willing, Lord

I have already told you how I was in Jerusalem when one night I was awakened suddenly. I have told you some of what the Lord told me. Here is the complete message that the Lord spoke to my heart in the wee hours of the morning:

"It is also past midnight in prophetic time. Listen to Me. One of My greatest concerns is that My people, part of My Church, do not suffer death by starvation before I return. Will you help feed them? To them it would be an angelic food supply! It would be a miracle! I say to you, hunger is an agonizing death. Give to those who are dying, and you shall live happily and victoriously.

"I speak to you in Jerusalem, the city where I took bread and blessed it and said, 'Take, eat, this is My body broken for you.' So take bread for the spirit, soul and body to the multitudes of the earth. Go especially to war areas where there is devastation and hunger, and feed them. Many are suffering.

"You will bring food in fast by plane. You will ride the plane, watch it given out and rejoice to see the children fed. Give food to refugees who will be coming to Israel who require help. It is My pity on them. America has the food. Buy it and take it to the hungry. Use storage houses to hold the food until you are ready to distribute it to the hungry.

"If I bless you financially for your needs, will you operate a global feeding program — only for My people? You will distribute the food through My churches only.

Around the world I want you to feed My hungry people. Don't let My people die of starvation.''

My response at 5:00 A.M., after listening to the Lord talk for over five hours, was, ''I am willing Lord.''

The Holy Spirit impressed upon me that we must use a three-pronged, aggressive attack against the forces of evil:

* feeding the hungry
* strengthening churches with pastors' seminars
* proclaiming the Gospel to the masses through evangelistic crusades.

The Lord promised me that He would raise up pastors and laymen who would miraculously support the Feed the Hungry program, and He has been faithful to His Word. The End-Time Joseph Program sponsored by my ministry has board members representing major churches in all parts of the world, and we respond quickly to the needs of people around the world.

The world has changed dramatically since the day when I started out as a seventeen-year-old boy to fulfill the call of God on my life. For years, the soles of my feet slapped the streets of the great cities and small villages of the world as I preached the Word of God, salvation, deliverance and healing in over one hundred nations and in over one thousand of the world's cities.

From the beginning, Jesus called me and gave me a simple promise that He was sending me to bear fruit that remains and that He would go with me and provide every need. I have proved Him for over sixty years of active ministry, and the more I do, the more He gives me to do.

I Pass the Sword to You

The sword I am passing to you is a sword that was passed to me. It may have come through the hands of Smith

Wigglesworth and Howard Carter, but it came from the Lord Jesus Himself Who said:

> ... **"All authority in heaven and on earth has been given to me. Therefore go and make disciples..., baptizing..., and teaching them to obey....And surely I am with you always, to the very end of the age."**
>
> **Matthew 28:18-20** NIV

Why did Jesus promise to be with you to the very end of the age if He did not expect you to continue going, making disciples, baptizing and teaching to the very end of the age — or at least to the end of your age (life span)?

The authority behind the Great Commission is Jesus. The authority behind the promise to be with you is Jesus. The authority behind your calling and anointing is Jesus. And, ...**God's gifts and his call are irrevocable** (Rom. 11:29 NIV).

Are you ready to receive the sword I am passing to you? Then receive it, and never release it — "to the very end of the age!"

27

In the Presence of Greatness

In Cardiff, Wales, before I returned to the United States, I was privileged to make friends with that legendary giant of the faith, Smith Wigglesworth, a renowned author whose writings are used as college texts today.

His was a miracle-studded ministry and the faith of Elijah. I was twenty-two and he was in his eighties. I visited him in his home in Bradford, Yorkshire, many times. During this time he told me much about his life and ministry, and the secrets of his great faith. He spent much time reading the Word of God, once issuing a challenge to anyone who could catch him without a copy of the Bible on him. He also said that he danced before the Lord for ten minutes every morning.

I asked him at one point why I never saw him down or depressed. He said that when he got up every morning he never asked Smith Wigglesworth how he felt, but praised God, danced before Him and looked to the Word of God for his direction and response.

On my final visit before returning to America, he said, "I am going to bless you with my spirit." We knelt, and he placed his hands on my shoulders and prayed: "God, let the faith that is in my heart be poured into the heart of this young man. And let the works that I have seen You do be done in his life and ministry. Let the blessing that You have given to me be his. Let the holy anointing that has rested upon my life rest upon his life."

I knew then that a new dimension of power would be evident in my life and ministry. I learned much about faith from Smith Wigglesworth, but the greatest benefit of my association with him was the spiritual impartation he gave me which has remained with me and shaped my life and ministry.

After leaving Smith Wigglesworth in England, Howard Carter and I took a boat to Canada. Six months later we went to Brazil, Bolivia, Portugal, Switzerland, Belgium, France and Germany. While soldiers marched and guns roared and the world prepared for World War II, we planted indigenous churches and helped them become national organisms to bring Christ to the nations.

I Pass the Sword to You

You probably never met Smith Wigglesworth or Howard Carter. But you have met people with faith, anointing and ministry who encouraged you and challenged you. Identify those men of God who have been placed into your life as role models, examples and teachers. Listen to them. Take notes on their sermons and learn from their ministry. Talk with them. Let them counsel you and pray with you.

Remember what Jesus said about Mary when she sat at His feet, listening to His every word? **But one thing is needful: and Mary hath chosen that good part, which shall not be taken away from her** (Luke 10:42). Continue to choose the good from those whom the Lord has placed in your life. That's what is needful for you, or the Lord would not have placed them into your life. Choose the good and glean from their lives. It shall not be taken away from you.

Now, go with God! He wants you!

I pass the sword to you.

Appendix

What Other Ministers Are Saying About Dr. Sumrall and This Book*

Dr. Sumrall has encouraged me as a young minister. His genuine interest in my life and calling has caused me to rise higher in my expectations of God's destiny for my life. His energy in serving the Lord is amazing.

Billy Joe Daugherty, Pastor
Victory Christian Center
Tulsa, Oklahoma

The one thing I've learned most from Dr. Sumrall is "focus." He is one of the most focused men I have ever met. Nothing clouds, diffuses or detracts him from his original vision. Years ago he told me, "Son, find out what it is God has anointed you to do and do it until you die. Plan your ministry for the long haul, and don't be in a big hurry to reach your peak."

Dick Bernal, Senior Pastor
Jubilee Christian Center
San Jose, California

I have known Brother Sumrall over a period of almost ten years. His wealth of experience has always inspired me, but most of all his absolute devotion and dedication to God's call on his life have been an awesome reminder of Who we serve. He can motivate and exhort Christians. He always

183

has a challenging word for fellow ministers, and, like distinguished men of God, leads by example. His sheer capacity for the work of the ministry leaves many a younger man panting in the dust.

Ray McCauley
Rhema Ministries
South Africa

As I travel around the nation, I constantly come face to face with someone who has been touched by Dr. Sumrall's ministry. Those who tell of their experiences while in his meetings, those who tell of lives changed because of a book. Those who are inspired by a telecast of his, and those who are changed and touched by his love for the multitudes. I hear these words continuously about this man of destiny, yet my heart always races back to a fonder memory of him in my life.

There was a time in my personal life that it appeared as if Satan had the final victory. I saw no light at the end of the tunnel, and I wasn't especially interested in trying to find it. Even hope's last glimmer couldn't be seen, and heartache was flooding over every footstep I made.

But Dr. Sumrall saw a hurting man snatching for help. I walked into my office one day only to find a note that Dr. Sumrall had left lying on my desk from the previous night's visit to my church. Scrawled affectionately across the paper were the words, "You can't go in reverse or the devil will have you!" Because of those words, things didn't look so hopeless or so overwhelming. They were written by a man who knew what it was to look hopelessness in the face and laugh!

Yes, I love the books, I soak up the teachings, I am moved by the preaching, and inspired by the integrity; but Dr. Sumrall, your love and compassion for the ministers of God and His children is what I can't help but see.

Ed Dufresne

Lester Sumrall, my beloved and esteemed friend in the Lord's great World Harvest, has been a constant in my life. I first met him in the 1950s and came to see who he is in the Lord — a mighty anointed prophet for our day. Since then we have been together in the United States and overseas countless times.

Lester Sumrall is called.

He is anointed and sent.

He is discerning of evil spirits.

He calls healing upon the sick.

He brings souls by the thousands to Christ.

He builds churches.

He extends the boundaries of the Kingdom.

He builds TV networks.

He publishes the Gospel.

He feeds the poor.

He lives Jesus twenty-four hours a day.

He is a pioneer of pioneers.

He is a lover of men.

To Lester and Louise, Evelyn and I, Richard and Lindsay, *love you.* You are dear to us.

Oral Roberts

Dr. Lester Sumrall has been a personal inspiration and blessing to me, especially in the area of stamina. He climbs God's mountains and reaches peak after peak. He is so good to give of his time to pastors like me. He is a challenge to the future for us.

Age M. Aleskjaer, Pastor
Oslo, Norway

I believe with all my heart in the ministry and the leadership of Dr. Lester Sumrall. I was a young man in 1959, a young Jewish orphan boy in my early twenties. Lester took me to the nations of the world. It was my second overseas trip.

When I came in contact with Dr. Sumrall's life and ministry, he saw in me an anointing of God and urged me to go to the nations of the world. He was the first one to do so, and it was through his life and influence that I went to the Philippines and Hong Kong — I will never forget it.

He was the one who encouraged me. I was just a little youngster wet behind the ears. I will never forget the trepidation and the fear I had in going out into that public meeting in the Philippine Islands. He would come into my room and slip his arm around me and pray with me before I would go out and face that field full of tens of thousands of people. I believe in his life, in his leadership, his ministry and his spirit of unselfishness.

Lester Sumrall opened up my heart to world missionary enterprise. He taught me when I was a young man to go to the mission field and took me out to the nations for Christ.
Morris Cerullo, Evangelist

Dr. Sumrall, there are so many things I sense, not just from the pulpit, but by being around you. Of course, the preaching, and the anointing on your life, but also just being around you. To see that your life is consistent has had a big, big effect on my life and ministry. I am forever thankful to God for that, and for what you have deposited here in Sweden.

Often when I make a decision and many times when I think about things, I feel the Spirit of God just remind me of how you do things or things you have said. I think you have a way of saying things that makes people remember it. Sometimes ministers just talk and talk and no one remembers at all what they say; they just waste their time. But it is something when you speak to young ministers.

The strength and power of your ministry needs to be shared to the next generation. What God has done through the nineteenth century is very important for young ministers to know about.

Ulf Ekman, Pastor
Uppsala, Sweden

---

*Personal testimonies were slightly edited for clarity.

Dr. Lester Sumrall is founder and chairman of a worldwide missionary outreach, The Lester Sumrall Evangelistic Association (LeSEA). Respected through-out the world as a missionary statesman, Dr. Sumrall has raised up churches and taught the Word of God for more than sixty years. In addition, he maintains headquarters for LeSEA Global and  LeSEA Broadcasting (international radio and television) in South Bend, Indiana, where he resides with his wife, Louise, and pastors Christian Center Cathedral of Praise. His three married sons, Frank, Stephen and Peter are also involved in the ministry.

Dr. Sumrall, a prolific author, has written more than 110 books and teaching syllabi. Besides his writing, he is founder and president of World Harvest Bible College and television host on ''LeSEA Alive'' and ''The Lester Sumrall Teaching Series.''

A powerful and dynamic speaker, Dr. Sumrall ministers God's message with authority and takes advantage of electronic media to reach the world today. He founded LeSEA Broadcasting, Inc., which owns and operates eight television stations in the following cities:

WHMB TV-40 Indianapolis, Indiana

WHME TV-46 South Bend, Indiana

KWHB TV-47 Tulsa, Oklahoma

KWHE TV-14 Honolulu, Hawaii

WHKE TV-55 Kenosha, Wisconsin

KWHD TV-53 Denver, Colorado

KWHH TV-14 Hilo, Hawaii

K21AG TV-21 Maui, Hawaii

A recent outreach to the world's hungry has thrust Dr. Sumrall into a new dimension of showing compassion to the far corners of the earth in response to our Lord's command to "feed the hungry." Called the End Time Joseph Program to Feed the Hungry, Dr. Sumrall is enlisting worldwide pastor-to-pastor support of this program. It is his belief that government alone should not shoulder the responsibility of caring for the world's homeless, hungry and needy, but that the Church is to be a responsible vehicle of Christ to suffering humanity.

To receive Lester Sumrall's monthly
magazine, *World Harvest*, write:

Lester Sumrall
P. O. Box 12
South Bend, Indiana 46624

*Please include your prayer requests
and comments when you write.*

Receive **the Sword**
at Lester Sumrall's World Harvest Bible College.
For a free catalogue about WHBC
or correspondence studies, write:

World Harvest Bible College
Box 12
South Bend, Indiana 46624

Other Books by Lester Sumrall

The Militant Church
Overcoming Compulsive Desires
101 Questions and Answers on Demon Powers
How to Cope Series:
Depression
Loneliness
Rejection
Suicide
Worry
Living Free
Miracles Don't Just Happen
Demons: The Answer Book
Run With the Vision
Ecstasy
Cup of Life
The Face of Jesus
The True Story of Clarita Villanueva
Destroying Your Deadliest Enemy
Seven Ways Jesus Healed the People

Available from your local bookstore or by writing:

Harrison House
P.O. Box 35035
Tulsa, Oklahoma 74153

In Canada contact: Word Alive • P. O. Box 284
Niverville, Manitoba • CANADA R0A 1E0

For international sales in Europe, contact:

Harrison House Europe • Belruptstrasse 42 A
A — 6900 Bregenz • AUSTRIA

The Harrison House Vision

Proclaiming the truth and the power
Of the Gospel of Jesus Christ
With excellence;

Challenging Christians to
Live victoriously,
Grow spiritually,
Know God intimately.